I0154087

Supermindful

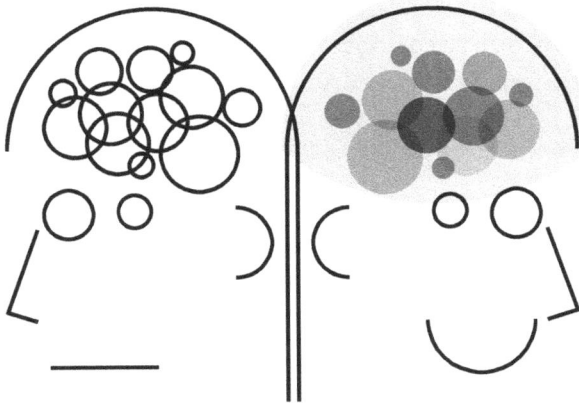

How to tap into your creativity

ELIZA LAY RYAN

Supermindful

First published in 2020 by

Panoma Press Ltd
48 St Vincent Drive, St Albans, Herts, AL1 5SJ, UK
info@panomapress.com
www.panomapress.com

Book layout by Neil Coe.

978-1-784521-70-7

The right of Eliza Ryan to be identified as the author of this work has been asserted in accordance with sections 77 and 78 of the Copyright, Designs and Patents Act 1988.

A CIP catalogue record for this book is available from the British Library.

All rights reserved. No part of this book may be reproduced in any material form (including photocopying or storing in any medium by electronic means and whether or not transiently or incidentally to some other use of this publication) without the written permission of the copyright holder except in accordance with the provisions of the Copyright, Designs and Patents Act 1988. Applications for the copyright holder's written permission to reproduce any part of this publication should be addressed to the publishers.

This book is available online and in bookstores.

Copyright 2019 Eliza Ryan.

To C. ~ a constant source of nourishing wonder

Contents

KNOW

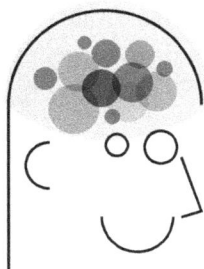

We Need to Be Able to See Differently

You live in a volatile, uncertain, chaotic, and ambiguous world.

Hooray!!

Hooray?

Do you feel glad?

No.

We are stressed out. Other people's behaviors worry us. New ideas seem scary. It's tough to get out of our well-worn grooves of thinking and reacting (even when we want to). And we feel badly about all of that. Which stresses us out more.

But really, it's not our fault. We feel stress because our brains are responding in the way they are supposed to respond when we feel unsafe—either fighting, fleeing, or freezing.

So, the feeling of stress really means that our brains are doing their jobs.

Well done brain?

What this means is that when we encounter something or someone that makes us feel uncomfortable, we either get angry at it, run away from it, or ignore it. Those are our options.

Now, do those look like great choices? No, they don't look great to me either. This book hopes to give you some other possibilities.

But first, why are we all spending so much time yelling, running, and sticking our heads in the sand these days? One reason is that we live in a "VUCA" world: Volatile, Uncertain, Complex, Ambiguous. The U.S. Army War College coined the term in response to the growth of the internet causing us to be instantly connected to a huge global community.[1, 2]

It's still true. But more so.

Pretty much everything we encounter—people, ideas, our newsfeeds—is potentially VUCA.

This wasn't always the case.

We used to live in small communities with agreed upon ways of thinking and being. We pretty much knew what to expect as we went about our lives. Maybe the town gossip was annoying, but we weren't baffled by how she lived and thought.

Now things are different.

We could encounter anyone or any kind of idea at any moment. Who knows what the next person we need to collaborate with, meet with, or sit next to at Starbucks, will be like? Who knows what we'll see each time we pick up our phone? We are constantly asked to adapt to new ideas and ways of doing things.

Our bodies used to engage in fighting, fleeing, and freezing just once in a while, to keep us safe from invaders of our village, or unknown types of berries; safe from lions and tigers and bears—oh my.

Our brains were designed to keep us safe from newness and otherness—new or untested (by us) ways of thinking, feeling, and behaving—because whatever we have been doing has kept us alive so far.

After all, if it's not broke…

So, our brains are still trying to keep us safe, but the problem is that, in this VUCA world, this actually make us *less* safe.

Whether we are a team member, an educator, an entrepreneur, or a family member, we know that in order to survive (let alone thrive), we need to be able to be dynamic, responsive, and flexible while remaining authentic. This is, obviously, the opposite of lashing out, getting out, or numbing out.

So here we are, doing the thing that is supposed to keep us safe—reacting against ways of thinking and being that are uncommon to us or uncomfortable for us—but now it is making us not only less safe, but damaged.

How?

The constant nature of the newness and otherness we experience, whether it is in the form of knowledge, ideas, or different ways of being in the world, overwhelms us. We are surrounded. There is nowhere to go. There is volatility, uncertainty, complexity, and ambiguity, everywhere. It is the nature of a globalized society. But it is not so much the discomfort of cultures in conflict that is our problem, as it is the inescapable knowledge that every human—from those we live with, to those we work with, to those halfway around the world, to those next door—might see the world very differently from how we see it.

We can no longer rest blithely in the comfort of thinking that things are just the way they are, because every time we see our newsfeed (or maybe every time we go to work, or every time we enter our own kitchen), it is clear that someone else thinks life should be lived quite differently; then the next moment we encounter another person whose behavior, clothes, music, words, or disposition, indicates that life should be lived more differently still.

We cannot assume that anyone we encounter sees the world the way we do. In fact, we know that they don't.

But we are social beings. We need community to thrive. And thus far, community has meant a kind of sameness: shared goals, shared values, shared likes. That isn't necessarily what community means any more. In fact, it can't mean that any more because we know that, even when we look the same, we are each very different, nuanced, and unique.

This awareness of the amazing variety of perspectives has the potential to be a wonderful turn of events (as we'll see throughout the book), but without tools, it is mostly just uncomfortable.

Being bombarded with discomfort and being unable to handle that experience is one damaging aspect of living in the VUCA world without the tools to help us navigate it.

Another damaging VUCA side-effect is that fighting against, and running away from things makes our own world smaller and smaller. It cuts off our ability to collaborate, communicate, and create new possibilities.

This lack of creativity in how we think, feel, and see the world causes us to lose out on relationships, innovation, and opportunities simply because we don't know how to be curious when faced with the unfamiliar or that which we don't like.

So, what are we to do?

We have a brain that is trying to keep us safe by rejecting certain ways of being, but we need to be able to engage with different ways of being in order to flourish.

You have probably heard about mindfulness. (Maybe you're even sick of hearing about mindfulness. Don't worry. There are as many ways to "do mindfulness" as there are to "do exercise," and for the sorts of mindfulness we will be exploring you don't even have to close your eyes.)

Foundationally, all mindfulness is, is paying attention to the present moment on purpose, and with curiosity. That's all.

By noticing life in this way, we are inside the flow of our experience while witnessing our experience. This gives us a little gap between what happens and how we respond to it. Choice—new ideas and responses—has a chance to emerge.

But where will all of those new ideas and responses come from?

As Einstein said: "Everyone sits in the prison of his own ideas."[3]

How can we have choice if we only have access to the ideas and the mind-set we already have?

Clearly, we need something else in order to succeed in gaining the dynamic, responsive fluidity we desire to navigate this VUCA world.

We need supermindfulness.

And that's what this book is all about.

What is supermindfulness?

Supermindfulness is the ability to be present to the moment as it is, as we are, while also being able to see that moment in new ways—to mine it for more possibilities.

It is awareness and flexibility.

And where do you find this flexibility?

Enter, acting techniques.

Acting techniques are nothing more than flexibility-building practices. They allow us to stand in someone else's shoes, real or imaginary. They allow us to shift perspective not just intellectually, but experientially.

They also teach us to cultivate the ability to shine our flashlight of awareness where we would like it to go, and become better able to be present with the moment—as we are, as it is—in the same way that traditional mindfulness practices do, but with eyes wide open inside the flow of life.

They allow us to be present and participating.

Having taught acting—both possibility and presence practices–to hundreds of actors and non-actors from all over the world (some students took the intensives for confidence building, public speaking, fun, etc.), my students continually report how much learning these flexibility shifting and presence fostering tools impacts their lives. Initially I taught just in the acting space, but now I teach these tools to people in business, education, and wellness as well.

The tools have expanded into these other spaces, because in my first years of teaching, when I was just teaching acting techniques in an acting context, students wrote to me:

"More than an acting class, it was a life class, getting to know ourselves in a way we never imagined."

"It is amazing how a few exercises... can make you understand things and even understand other people and relate with them, even if they're strangers."

"I entered in class to become a better actor and I went out a better person."

Initially their feedback surprised me. I knew that *acting* could facilitate those sorts of experiences. As Sally Field put it:

> I find that's one of the great things about acting—you have the opportunity to stand in somebody else's shoes... and as an actor you're able to step into that character's skin, look through her eyes. You leave transformed, a different person, because once you live a little bit of someone's life, it changes you.[4]

But I wasn't teaching acting. The students weren't interpreting characters in my class. They were just learning tools and frameworks that would make interpreting characters—being present, standing in new shoes and seeing through new eyes—easier for them. As a byproduct, they noticed that these same tools helped them understand not just fictional people better, but real people as well, and even parts of themselves.

This was exciting because the kinds of acting techniques we were exploring are practices anyone can do anytime, anywhere. Why should it only be the people who've taken an acting class who get to learn these tools? Why should we only learn how to extend curiosity to fictional characters?

This all made sense, but I wanted to really understand the why and how of these techniques: why they work, and how they could work even better. Because, of course, it's harder to extend curiosity to real people—to allow real other people and real parts of ourselves that we dislike to spark creativity in us.

I dove into the psychological, social psychological, and neuroscientific research that I had been studying throughout my academic life and in my training as a yoga teacher. I collaborated with neurologists at Brigham and Women's Hospital/Harvard University to develop a mindfulness study, and with leaders in business, education, and wellness, to see what I could learn from them and where our work could cross-pollinate.

And through this exploration I discovered some interesting things.

Why do these particular practices that actors learn seem to work in everyday life to increase curiosity, creativity, and empathy? The answer emerges from the marriage of four ingredients:

- Knowledge
- Playfulness
- Awareness
- Imagination

Knowledge of why we do or don't shift perspective helps us understand what's getting in our way, so we don't blame ourselves. We see that the habits of how we and other people think and go about doing things are adaptive, and maybe even helpful as long as we know about them and treat them as if they are helpful.

Playfulness prevents the brain from getting scared of change, thus letting us experience new things. (The people in the acting class weren't trying to change themselves in a particular way, after all. That is important.)

Awareness, presence, allows us a better handle on how things are.

Imagination, possibilities, allows us to see how else things might be.

When each of these are present, new ways of being occur to us, and new or different ways of being seem less threatening.

In strengthening our ability to be present with what is as it is, and by learning how to be open to seeing how else things might be, we increase curiosity and decrease fear.

From moment to moment, we become better able to respond dynamically with the person or idea in front of us, which increases our social and intellectual agility. And as we become more attuned to our own experience, we are able to respond more authentically.

Last, all of this serves to connect us more to our intuition and our gut.

Increasing our ability to playfully experience different perspectives doesn't dilute or weaken our own—quite the opposite. In exploring different ways of seeing the world, we gain experiences that refine, deepen, and sharpen our own authentic reasoning.

The benefit of both acting techniques and traditional mindfulness is that they give our intuition more possibilities to choose from, making us more effortlessly and intelligently creative.

They are tools that allow us to shift our default mode from judgment and defensiveness to curiosity and wonder. Just the tools we need right now.

But why do we judge, and reject, and estrange ourselves from one another?

What has worked for us, has worked for us! We are still alive, aren't we? So, our "selves" aren't too keen on rocking the boat.

And what has worked for you *has* worked for you. You are fine. This is not a book about achieving perfection.

- There is no such thing as perfect.
- All ways of being have some intelligence. Our wholeness is our richness. Why would we want to collapse ourselves into one tiny box of an idea representing who we should be?

We are often told to focus on the positive and are warned that our thoughts become reality, so we'd better be careful what we think (and even what we feel). And, certainly, fostering good feelings, thoughts, and actions (whatever "good" means to us) can help us cultivate new and potentially better expressions of self. In fact, the exercises in this book are particularly helpful to these ends.

But what about these ideas: "I'm not good enough," or "I'm not smart enough," or "People don't like me." Those are normal thoughts too. When we decide that those ways of thinking are just bad or dangerous, we lose out, for several reasons.

When we assume that a way of being has no value, we can get no value from it.

For example, what if "people don't like me" wasn't something terrible but something liberating: "People don't like me anyway, so I am going to be how I want to be." Might that be a helpful way of being to have access to sometimes? Or just experiencing the pure, sad feeling of "people don't like me" might teach us how much we need and want other people, causing us to value them more. Or it could help us feel compassion for those left out of the social center. Or it could help us better understand the reason someone lashes out from a place of isolated anger.

Rejecting a way of being as simply being bad or dangerous makes it impossible for us to understand someone who experiences the world that way. This carries two costs.

Simply rejecting a way of being, and thereby the people who are that way, and looking no further at it, cuts us off from collaborative possibilities. This is a huge cost to pay in every social setting from the workplace to citizenship.

Furthermore, we will encounter people (and even aspects of our own selves) who harbor some of these disapproved of feelings and beliefs. When we say "bad and wrong," and leave it at that, we miss out on engaging with the factors giving rise to what we don't like. As a result, we don't learn or move forward in any way toward the goal we'd like to see actualized.

Might it be helpful to reach toward understanding, so we can attempt to make forward progress instead of grumbling to ourselves with no change in sight?

Not that grumbling is a problem. That is adaptively intelligent too. Grumbling is very helpful! It tells us what we don't like. It helps to alert us that something is wrong for us.

The question here is not: "What's the best way to be?" The question is: "What's the most useful way to be in any particular moment?"

How does supermindfulness help give us this ability to respond dynamically instead of habitually?

Here is one example:

I had a student, an ebullient rapper from China, who went to the restroom on a class break. We had been working on shifting perspectives with physicality. And he came back very excited. He said that he had *really* needed to go to the bathroom, but when he got there, this woman was in there cleaning, and she kind of scowled at him when he tried to come in, which made him mad. Normally, he said, he would have barked at her to leave. But then he looked at her.

He saw that her shoulders were curved in, her brow was furrowed, and her mouth was turned down. Without even trying, he noticed that he naturally took on her physicality for a split second—and felt sad. She wasn't trying to be difficult. She was very sad.

He said: "Hi, how are you?"

She responded with words that said "fine," but in a tone that said "not fine."

He thought: "Am I going to yell at a sad stranger?" Instead, he smiled at her, wished her a good day, and went to find another bathroom. He felt elated. A feeling he probably wouldn't have had if he'd scowled back at the scowling woman.

The student's heightened awareness of the person in front of him, and his ability to experience a feeling on purpose—one we would normally label as negative, or bad (sadness)—ultimately gave him greater joy because it gave him a choice in how he responded to life.

This wasn't a taxing choice. It was an intuitive, yet conscious response that could happen effortlessly. He had developed greater curiosity, awareness, and flexibility. Because of this, he could respond both more dynamically and more authentically to what was happening.

Actors (and scientists, athletes, business leaders, and parents) know that in the moment of dynamic, creative engagement, they are not making mental calculations. They are relying on a well-informed intuition to respond intelligently to what is happening.

Alan Turing, the father of the computer, wrote:

> [R]easoning may be regarded… as the exercise of a combination of two faculties, which we may call intuition and ingenuity. The activity of the intuition consists in making spontaneous judgments which are not the result of conscious trains of reasoning. These judgments are often but by no means invariably correct… The exercise of ingenuity… consists in aiding the intuition through suitable arrangements of propositions... when these are really well arranged the validity of the intuitive steps which are required cannot seriously be doubted.[5]

Here Turing is discussing mathematical reasoning, but his logic can apply to any reasoning. Turing had to study math in order for his ingenuity to be able to aid his intuition in that sphere. He had to develop a fluency in mathematical propositions.

In the same way that Alan Turing exercised his fluency in mathematics, resulting in his intuition and ingenuity working together to create the first computer, we can exercise our fluency in the ways that we and other people think, feel, and behave.

By doing this we can then have greater intuition and ingenuity in creating our lives, relationships, and societies.

And it is not optional, but necessary that we exercise this fluency in different ways of being. Especially in our current world.

If our intuition is informed only by our genetics and life experience, it is not a very well-informed intuition, is it? It doesn't have much to draw on that we've actually put there or are even aware of.

If we don't exercise our flexibility, our intuition has the habits it got by happenstance.

As Einstein noted: "Common sense is nothing more than a deposit of prejudices laid down in the mind before you reach eighteen."[6]

What the presence part of supermindfulness does is it allows us to stop for a moment and notice how our life experience has bumped up against our genetics. It helps us ask: "How are we seeing or experiencing this moment?" It allows us to find a point of stillness where we can see what's happening right now, just as it is. Not oming-unruffled-on-a-mountaintop, just greater awareness.

Increasing your flexibility allows you to experience how *else* you might see any moment you are in, not because that way would be better, but because:

- It is fun for the brain to experience new things on purpose. (The feel-good neurotransmitter dopamine gets released.)[7]

- Having experienced another way of being will come in handy because, having experienced it yourself, it won't seem so foreign to you. This means you will more easily interact with this way of being when it presents itself in other people.

- Your intuition will have more to draw on than just your habits the next time a situation comes up where a different way of being might be helpful. (And because it is *your* intuition that is using the new way of being, you will still be authentically *you*—just more of you.)

We can explore new possibilities of perspective on the level of our disposition, the level of our thoughts, or the level of our actions. And we can do this subtly so that nobody is aware of our practicing their use.

I have spent much of my time teaching film acting, and film actors cannot express anything in an exaggerated way or they look ridiculous (as you know from watching them), so these are merely shifts of thought.

Go ahead and think "I love!" Notice how that feels. Look at the room you are in. Notice what you notice. Now go ahead and think "I hate!" Notice how that feels. Look at the room you are in. Notice what you notice.

Through shifting thoughts, dispositions, and actions, we condition ourselves to be internally flexible: the way athletes condition themselves to be physically flexible. Presence then serves the function of strength training, stabilizing and integrating that flexibility so we can use it spontaneously.

To play around with possibilities, we can use two readily available sources of inspiration:

- Invention
- Observation

Actors strengthen their powers of observation and their powers of invention in order to increase their ability to think, feel, and do things in more ways, and to experience any character's perspective.

We can all do this—we can experience any perspective, or at the very least, reach toward experiencing.

As we've seen, to support this interplay of agility and authenticity, to support our ability to cultivate supermindfulness, we have the ingredients of awareness, imagination, playfulness, and knowledge.

The first part of the book deals with knowledge. We'll look at why it is usually hard to shift perspective and how it can be easier and fun.

In the Knowledge part of the book, we will draw on psychological research and other sources to understand how we tend to think, feel, relate to other people, and create habits. We will look at what makes it difficult, and what makes it easy for us to shift how we think, feel, and behave.

The second part of the book contains 52 presence and possibilities exercises—52 ways to wonder—to help you cultivate supermindfulness. They will help you practice experiencing more and more ways of igniting greater curiosity, empathy, and creativity in the flow of your daily life.

But It Can Be Difficult to Shift Perspective

The Weight of Information

As we've already noted, the world wasn't always so VUCA in this particular way. It was VUCA in other ways: droughts, wars, plagues, and shifting empires are factors that all cause us to feel the pressure that life is volatile, uncertain, complex, and ambiguous.[8]

But we weren't always so rapidly connected. We didn't always have so much newness, otherness, different forms of idealness, or information to absorb.

Our awareness of, and engagement with, the infinite possible ways of thinking, feeling, expressing, and behaving that people can have, has sent us into a kind of existential spiral where we know that our version of reality isn't the only version of reality, but we don't know how to hold more than one version and let them inter-inform each other (or go deeper to access what might be truly universal).

Even when we try to include more perspectives, we often fail because our desire to feel stable is so strong, and (thus far) stability has meant having our own norms affirmed and protected. So, this is our challenge: our ultra-connected environment forces us to realize how interconnected we are, but everyone has different norms they are trying to affirm, and protect, against the threatening pull of that web of interconnectedness. Competing norms are one of the challenges facing us as we relate to our own VUCA moment.

Another challenge is the sheer volume of information. In other historical moments, there was less complexity because there was less information. News traveled much more slowly and sparingly— so did we. We had time to digest not only information but also the scenery as we moved through our lives.

Things are different now.

As the character Marilyn, in the play *David's RedHaired Death*, by Sherry Kramer, says (first produced in the same year that the term VUCA emerged):

> There was a time a person had only a hundred deaths, at best. In remote, isolated places forty or fifty had to do. When a man died, the only people who had his death were the members of his family, and those close enough to know him, day by day. And so consequently, no one ever went through life carrying the weight of more than several dozen deaths on top of them. We have death differently now. The sheer volume of death in the global village demands it… There

are so, so many people in the world. All having deaths, over and over. We are not far away, I'm afraid, from a moment of critical mass, of geometric progression, when we are all carrying so many deaths that the system must collapse, like a black hole, must just consume itself in its own weight.[9]

Now movement and change are rapid and constant. Now we have, not only more deaths but also more information at our fingertips than we could digest in infinite lifetimes—much of it shocking and baffling to us. Why is he saying that? Why is she proposing that? Why is he doing that? What is that about? It is no wonder that addiction is rising, as we try to cope with the sense of overwhelm and disconnection by numbing ourselves at ever higher rates.[10]

For our own health and wellbeing, we need to learn how to allow the differences and newness we encounter to ignite our curiosity, instead of our ire, by tapping into our sense of a shared humanity, our own integrity, and our imaginations.

In a multinational, longitudinal study, psychiatrist and researcher C. Robert Cloninger found that three character traits working together predicted the "best health, most friends, fewest emotional problems and greatest satisfaction with life" in people.

These three traits were novelty-seeking, persistence, and self-transcendence. In other words, the desire to seek out new experiences, the ability to persist by "regulat[ing] your impulses while also having the imagination to see what the future would be like if you tried something new," and "the capacity to get lost in the moment doing what you love to do, to feel a connection to nature and humanity and the universe." [11, 12]

Supermindfulness, presence, and possibilities working in concert, all help strengthen these traits.

We need to be able to support these aspects of ourselves in order to find it fun and nourishing, instead of totally overwhelming, to engage with all of this information; to investigate people's motives and understand the needs driving behavior so we can work with, live with, and society-build with people who are different from us.

It is possible to expand to include new ways of being without losing the way we are.

In fact, through imaginative expansion, we can become even more ourselves, as Annette Benning explains: "One of the pleasures of acting is that every time we get to enter this other imaginative world that's not our own... it's such a fabulous way to expand your own heart and your own thinking."[13]

Learning to slow down and be present, and learning how to open ourselves to see what else is there expands us, because it attunes us to the fact that everyone is a specific person, in a specific context, with a specific history. Everyone has an inner life that causes their actions to feel necessary to them (including us). Knowing this, and engaging with this reality, gives actors practice in seeing in a more four-dimensional way—a way we can all practice seeing.

Instead of actions and words happening in a vacuum, they happen in relationship to institutions, cultures, and other specific people, and they are born of that person's life experience. No person is just one thing. And no person exists outside multiple contexts.

(And it is important to note that multiple factors also contribute to our current VUCA iteration that are beyond the scope of this book [economic, environmental, and political factors], but not beyond the scope of the book's tools. Actors use the practices you will be using to try to understand every aspect of the ecosystem their character is a part of. It is helpful to use these same tools to understand our own real-life context as well.)

In daily life, we tend to group people (including ourselves) into labeled buckets of rich, poor, from here, not from here; or into flattened traits such as anxious, mean, kind, nice, rather than seeing people and ourselves in this more specific, nuanced, and whole way.

Oftentimes the way we reduce people is by labeling them as crazy or idiotic. It is interesting, and potentially helpful, to note that the etymology of idiot is "ignorant" and the etymology of ignorant is "ignore." So, when we call someone an idiot, what we mean is they are ignoring information we think is important to know. Similarly, the etymology of crazy is "full of cracks." So, when we call someone crazy, we really mean their thinking has cracks and fissures. So, these words can be helpful if taken from this perspective. They point toward the possible positive actions of helping to fill in the gaps and helping to make connections for other people. (And looking to see where our own gaps and disconnects might be.)

Reducing people and ideas to their worst, most prevalent, or most unfamiliar trait is making us not only less safe but it's also hurting us. A lack of nuance and outright rejection results in an us-versus-them deadlock, which keeps us all trapped in our own preconceptions—and nothing new can happen. [14]

Of course, we engage in this reductionist thinking because the constant nature of the newness and discomfort of otherness we experience, whether in the form of ideas, actions, or norms, overwhelms us. We want to end it somehow, and that response is understandable and sometimes beneficial.

Fighting, running, and numbing can sometimes be good solutions. They are not problems as long as they are actually serving us. But flooding our own bodies with cortisol and adrenaline rarely helps us.

Again, here we have a brain that is trying to keep us safe by rejecting certain ways of being, but we need to be able to engage with, investigate, and explore all the ways of being in order to flourish in our current world.

To do that, we have to make exploring other ways of being fun for ourselves.

To do that we need to reignite our whole selves, all of our faculties, not just our thinking brains but our senses, our emotions, our imaginations—all of us.

We can do this through learning how to wonder again. To wonder is a verb, and that verb helps us to cultivate supermindfulness.

As Plato noted: "Wonder is the only beginning of wisdom."[15]

Or as the character Celie writes in Alice Walker's book, *The Color Purple*[16]:

> I think us here to wonder, myself. To wonder. To ast. And that in wondering bout the big things and asting bout the big things you learn about the little ones, almost by accident. But you never know noting more about the big things than you start out with. The more I wonder... the more I love.

To wonder is an action. It's something we can do.

When we imaginatively encounter a new way of being with our whole selves, in the way that people in an acting class learn to do, we are not just receiving cognitive data, we are having an experience. This experience provides us not only with more conceptual information but also with more possible ways of thinking, feeling, and responding, to choose from and use ourselves.

For example, right now, bring your awareness to your jaw—become present with your jaw. Now tighten your jaw. Notice how it feels to clench your jaw. How do you feel? What state of being are you in with your jaw clenched? What emotions do you feel? Now let it go, and let your mouth slightly open and release your jaw. How do you feel? What state of being are you in? What emotions do you feel?

One puts you on guard and makes you alert. The other relaxes you and dissipates attention. Both are helpful ways of being and both are ways of being we might encounter in someone else.

As you can see, playfully encountering life in this way is not some arduous mental task. It is a reincorporation of our whole selves into our whole lives, and it is how we learn best, naturally.

As the father of modern acting Konstantin Stanislavski said: "In the language of an actor, to *know* is synonymous with to *feel*."[17]

We have to feel something to really understand it. Feeling can be vulnerable in the short term, but it is the only way to access our actual experience—to see what is actually occurring for us. The cost of trying not to feel is the fear and stress that currently buries us. We can try not to feel, but we are still feeling, so those emotions become an overwhelming sensation of anxiety as opposed to packets of information that we can learn from.

Leaning into feeling doesn't mean that we bombard ourselves with discomfort. No. This is where playfulness and presence come in. Playfulness and presence together help wondering feel less vulnerable. They allow us to get a better handle on what seems like an otherwise overwhelming barrage of emotional sensations.

When we force ourselves to experience new ways of being, or our own feelings, we increase our stress. Just reading (and writing) that sentence "force ourselves to experience" is stressful!

Instead, we need to create an atmosphere of safety and playfulness for ourselves. A state where we *want* to experience, where we *want* to feel, where our whole selves feel safe showing up to experience life as it is, and as it might be.

Presence, holding our own experience with compassion, acceptance, and care all allow us to root down into our own experience, and to honor the pre-existing wisdom that we hold. It allows us to see how the coping mechanisms we've developed work for us, and to see how truly capable we are.

By practicing presence, we practice affirming our experience while holding it loosely at the same time, so we can see it, handle it, and understand it. Instead of trying to change it and make it into what we think we want it to be, we can wonder about it. We can invite a spirit of playfulness around it. And *then*, from that resourced, stable place, we can branch out to see what other ways of being might be possible.

When we feel safe enough, we can open up to new possible experiences, then switch back to being present, then back to new possibilities. We visit the status quo and then visit the place of imagination. In this way the two can inter-inform each other and yield creativity, innovation, and maybe even wisdom.

Luckily, despite its desire to maintain the status quo, given an environment of safety and play, our brains crave new sensations, new experiences, and novelty.

Most of us don't like to be blindsided, but when we encounter newness in a safe-feeling environment, it feels good to us and we want to do it more. (This is one reason the internet and television can be so addictive. They provide us newness from a safe distance.)[18] In fact, the brain is really a novelty-seeking machine (some people's more than others').[19] It seeks new stimuli (images, sounds, stories, tastes, textures). It wants to explore the external world. It just doesn't necessarily want to always explore the internal world of the external world.

However, through employing the techniques actors use, new ways of thinking, feeling, and behaving become the fun, novel stimuli we crave. What might otherwise feel threatening, now feels exciting and fun when we engage it as playful stimuli, instead of something to merely like or dislike.

We can feed our brain the novelty it desires inside the flow of life, by turning the people, ideas, and situations we encounter into catalysts for our own curiosity. In doing so, we turn the otherwise stressful world around us into a playground where we are constantly learning and growing.[20, 21, 22]

As we've noted, these practices allow us to engage with different ways of being not only cognitively but emotionally. Cognitive plus emotional engagement is what enables us to make longer-term memories,[23, 24] to move what we learn from working memory to stored memory. When we engage a way of thinking, feeling, or being with our whole selves, we really learn from it, so when we encounter it later, we can respond more easily with intuitive effortlessness. We don't have to think about it. It's there for us.

As an article on business decisions from MIT Sloan School of Management points out, a well-informed intuition is key for navigating VUCA-land. The authors write:

> The more extensive a decision maker's experience, the more patterns he or she will be familiar with; the more patterns, the better the intuition. When an experienced senior executive attributes a decision to "gut instinct," he is saying in different words that he recognizes patterns from experience.[25]

We want to have access to more intuitively excellent judgments, not just in business and acting but also in everyday life.

So, this is all very practical. If, *inside of the context of our ability to generate safety and playfulness for ourselves*, we head toward what is unknown or "other" to us—what makes people and ideas (and parts of ourselves) seem stressful—then those things become known. They no longer seem so VUCA. In fact, ideas that once seemed threatening can become creative fodder.

The VUCA world becomes our greatest creative asset.

James Dean put this another way: "An actor must interpret life, and in order to do so must be willing to accept all the experiences life has to offer. In fact, he must seek out more of life than life has put at his feet."[26]

This orientation toward curiosity can be useful to anyone.

Why should actors have all the fun when we can all "seek out more of life"?

But why don't we?

The Brain's Short Cuts

What we think and how we tend to feel about people and ideas are filtered through habits, cultural norms, our immediate experiences, and our past experiences, which, far from being objective or universal, are unique to us.

These are helpful short cuts the brain takes so we can efficiently go about our lives. They also create huge blind spots for us in how we relate to other people, ideas, and even aspects of ourselves.

Actors need to think about these influences when faced with a character's backstory—the facts of a fictional person's life—in order to make sure they aren't imposing their own preconceptions onto the character. They have to (or get to, depending on how you look at it) become aware of their own biases because they know that we all make quick and dirty judgments about other people— real and fictional—that can either obscure or inform our view of them, depending on how aware we are.

We can all think about these biases when faced with anyone's backstory to help reveal information that we otherwise would miss, because the inability to see other people clearly has huge consequences.

We quickly form judgments about someone else's most salient features. One frequently used list is: [27]

1. Education Level

2. Economic Level

3. Perceived Credibility, Believability, Competence and Honesty

4. Trustworthiness

5. Level of Sophistication

6. Sex Role Identification

7. Level of Success

8. Political Background

9. Religious Background

10. Ethnic Background

11. Social/Professional/Sexual Desirability

That person then spends the rest of their relationship with us trying to disprove our wrong assumptions (if they can even figure out what those wrong assumptions are). And this is an uphill battle for them because we tend to look for evidence to corroborate our beliefs, ignoring evidence to the contrary.[28]

As an example: to one person "Robert went to Harvard" could mean "Robert is brilliant"; to another "Robert is rich"; to another "Robert tests well"; to another "Robert is stuck up"; all before ever even meeting Robert. If we don't know what "Robert went to Harvard" means to us, when we do meet poor Robert, we might not see him at all. He will be spending his time (unwittingly) proving our own preconceptions to ourselves. While we will be spending our time (unwittingly) proving his assumptions about us.

Let's Do an Experiment

Let's see what your assumptions are about someone based on these facts. Look at each one and see what words, feelings, thoughts, images, or associations come to mind.

34

Male

European

Incarcerated

Previously homeless

High school education

Artist

Military

Christian

So, we have a 34-year-old European, Christian male who is both an artist and a soldier. He has a high school education. He was homeless for a time and incarcerated for a time.

What do you think this person is like given these facts? What ideas do you have about how capable, or kind, or moral he might be? Just notice what you notice.

Now let's see how two fictional people, Buddy and Rachel, might view this same person based on the same facts. (Notice what assumptions the two names Buddy and Rachel spark for you too.)

Let's say Rachel makes meaning from those attributes this way:

34: still growing into maturity

Male: strong, sensitive

European: smart

Incarcerated: bad luck, not enough guidance

Previously homeless: unfortunate

High school education: smart

Artist: thoughtful, deep

Military: motivated

Christian: spiritual

Rachel's understanding, based on these facts, would be that of a not yet mature guy who was smart, thoughtful and talented. He was motivated to do well but had some bad luck and hadn't been guided well.

Let's look at what Buddy might think about Person X given the attributes:

34: adult

Male: logical and smart

European: sexy

Incarcerated: strong and bold

Previously homeless: lazy

High school education: unmotivated

Artist: wishy-washy

Military: scrappy

Christian: trustworthy

Buddy's understanding of Person X would be that of an adult who is a strong, smart, sexy, and deep yet scrappy, but also lazy around his own personal ambition.

Who is Person X?[1]

See how our natural tendency to make a snap judgment about someone else's wholeness can lead us astray?

So, our assumptions about what "facts" mean about certain people can get in the way of seeing what they are truly capable of.

But this is also where judgments become helpful. If we can recognize our snap-judgment biases and other habits and propose alternative possibilities to ourselves (as we did surrounding Hitler), then we can tease apart the threads of our blanket-statement-prone minds to see the pattern our thoughts are woven into. To mix metaphors: through awareness, once we can see them, our judgments can be seeds for creativity, new choices, and seeing things differently.

The brain's tendency to notice large changes and ignore small ones is another short cut, and an especially potent obfuscator of logic.

In one story about a tire company, from the book *Sacred Cows Make the Best Burgers*, a new employee was walking by the assembly line and asked why they wrap the tires in foil. The manager scoffed and explained condescendingly that the foil was there to protect the whitewalls on the tire from getting scratched. The employee pointed out that a very small percentage of tires still had whitewalls, and those that did were made of scuff-resistant rubber. His observation saved the company $22 million (in the 1980s).[29]

Over time small changes had added up to a big change that hadn't been noticed. This happens with individuals too. The more we grow familiar with shifting into different lenses, the easier it will be for us to spot the proverbial "foil on the tires" in our own lives, because we will be accustomed to questioning our assumptions. We will be in the habit of actively acquiring new possible ways of seeing a person, idea, or situation.

---

1   Adolf Hitler

Our "foil on the tires" might be an outdated way to see a spouse, child, or friend. It might be how we see our boss or co-worker. It might be how we see our careers, our company, or our department. It might be how we approach projects, learning, parenting, or being a friend or citizen.

The ability to see our own mind-sets and use that awareness productively is what allows for creative synthesis to yield new possibilities.

As an example, let's looks at the manager who was putting foil on the tires. We know from his action (putting the foil on) that he believed "everything's fine" in this area of the business. This was the lens he looked through.

This isn't a bad mind-set. It's a great one! Go ahead and adopt it. Really adopt "everything is fine" as your belief and thought. Notice how you feel when that is your mind-set. Look up and around. And notice what you notice around you. Ask yourself why: "Everything is fine. Why? Because…" Answer yourself and notice what you notice. We do this naturally. It is called confirmation bias, where we look for data that confirms our pre-existing predilections (as we saw when talking about "Robert at Harvard").

Did you notice how that belief allows you to notice what is actually fine in your immediate surroundings?

This mind-set allows us to be relaxed about what is happening. We aren't hyper-vigilantly scanning the landscape for problems, so a few details might slip by undetected, but our mental energy is free for us to use in the ways we'd like, or to deal with pressing issues.

For example, from this mind-set, I look up and I see that everything is fine because my computer is working, I have a cup of coffee next to me, and it is warm out. The air is soft and lovely. It is quiet. From this perspective, I can focus on the task that seems most important to me: writing.

But what about "something is wrong?" Let's adopt that mind-set to see what it gives us. Go ahead and really adopt it as your prevailing thought. "Something is wrong." Look up and around, notice how you feel. And notice what you notice around you. Ask yourself why: "Something is wrong. Why? Because…" Answer yourself and notice what you notice.

Do you see how it allows us to notice what is actually wrong? It allows us to become critical. That's great too.

For example, I look up and I see the napkin crumpled next to the coffee cup that needs to be thrown out, and then I think of how I should have done laundry last night so the cloth napkins would have been clean, which is better for the environment and more pleasant for me. I notice that my upper back is hurting a little, also I'm writing outside and there are thick clouds past the trees—it looks like rain. These are all things that I am going to need to address at some point (throwing the napkin out) or respond to (moving inside when the rain comes), and now I see them and am aware of them. Great! Helpful!

This mind-set might have helped the manager notice the foil.

If the employee had never existed, the manager could have saved the company that money by engaging both mind-sets of "everything is okay" and "something is wrong" together.

The new tire company employee, on the other hand, was not seeing through the lens of things being fine or being wrong. He had a different lens entirely, which is what allowed him to see the foil. What could it have been? We don't know.

But let's look at a possible inner monologue of the new employee: "I hope I don't mess up. I can't do this job. Who are we kidding? I don't know enough. No, no, I can, I can. Okay. Just look around and ask questions. It's okay to ask questions if I don't know something."

"Excuse me, why do we put foil around the tires?"

From this inner monologue we can identify two beliefs that this employee has: "I don't know if I'm capable" and "it's okay to not know everything."

In fact, it is the first belief that makes the second belief happen. The belief that it is okay to ask questions is a solution to the emotional problem created by the belief that he doesn't know enough.

It is not "something is right" or "something is wrong" that saves $22 million, but the belief (insecurity) "I don't know if I'm incapable" combined with (earnest pluckiness), "it's okay to ask questions."

This is what creative synthesis is. Our messy humanity in honest dialogue with itself:

"I am incapable" + "it's okay to ask questions" = $22 million savings.

Just choosing one belief or trying to strengthen the "best" beliefs is not how truly dynamic thinking works.

When we try to avoid problems or parts of ourselves, we miss out because problems and our full selves can be what lead to solutions.

We miss out on the call and response: the interplay of opposites that give rise to truly new possibilities.

Hidden Influences

Another unseen force that shapes our thoughts, feelings, actions, and judgments is our immediate environment and experience. If we don't have access to moment to moment awareness, then who knows what's making us think, feel, and do whatever we do?

A wonderful example of how immediate experiences shape our thoughts, feelings and actions but also can be mitigated by awareness is found in a classic study at Columbia University. [30]

Subjects were given epinephrine to give them an elevated mood (pounding heart, sweating, feeling over excited). Only half the people were told how they would feel. Each person was then put in a room with either an angry person or a euphoric person.

The people who weren't warned about side-effects became either angry or euphoric themselves, depending on which mood they were locked in with.

The people who were warned that they would feel elevated didn't change mood in response to the angry or euphoric person.

Both groups' feelings changed based on taking the epinephrine, but the uninformed group attributed their feelings to the wrong thing in thinking they were having actual emotions. The knowledgeable group did not. They knew that they were merely having a physical sensation.

We experience something similar in our own lives when we've had too much coffee, or not enough; too much food, or not enough; too much sleep, or not enough. And we don't even know what the other people we are encountering have just consumed or how much sleep they have or haven't had.

Actors call these factors "the given circumstances." These are the facts of the person's life and how those facts are affecting them emotionally, mentally, and behaviorally.

Each of us has given circumstances that affect us all the time. Our feelings, thoughts, and actions often flow from them. Our ability to be present in our feelings, and to our lives, helps us see how the given circumstances might be at play in ourselves, and in other people. And sometimes our given circumstances are someone else's!

I remember an experience where someone else's given circumstances became mine. I was 13 years old, and I went to the bank and was feeling excited and grown-up about going there by myself. I entered the building eager and fresh-faced, but the teller was in a snippy, dark mood. I noticed that, as I left the bank, I felt sad and angry, as if I were under a dark, stormy cloud. As I was on my way to see friends, I knew I'd carry the dark cloud with me, and I didn't want them to be infected with feelings that belonged to none of us. I had five blocks to transform my mood.

I remember being so relieved that I had noticed what I was feeling and why. It was also a fun and empowering game to fight the clock to dissipate the cloud.

Catching that bank teller's mood, I now know, is called "emotional contagion." People "catch" the feelings of one another, and the more we like someone the more we catch their feelings. Some people's moods are more contagious than others. Some people are more susceptible to catching moods, while some people are both.[31, 32]

One journal explains it like this:

> We unconsciously tend to mimic and synchronize our own nonverbal expressions with the nonverbal expressions of other people. Thus, we smile, frown, move, cry, sit, or stand in the same way as others, without necessarily being aware of our copying behavior. The bodily feedback from this mimicry would change our subjective feelings accordingly. In other words, we do not merely smile, or frown, but our smiling or frowning makes us feel happy, or angry, in accordance with these nonverbal displays.[33]

Emotional contagion can cause use to feel, think, and do many things we might or might not otherwise be inclined toward.

For example, soccer teams are more likely to both win the game and make the opposing team miss the next point, if the guy who scores the penalty kick throws his arms up in the air in celebration afterwards. His team catches his excitement about scoring, and on they go to victory.[34]

Or, parents who are more susceptible to feeling other peoples' feelings are more likely to "catch" their crying baby's distress, leading to an angry or even abusive response to their child's wailing. It's not that the parent means to get angry at their upset child. They catch the emotion, unconsciously join in the misery, and then—like putting an oxygen mask on yourself first in an airplane—they need to stop their own misery before they can attend to their child's.

In order to do that, they need to stop the source of the misery—the baby's crying. It is the baby's own upset (which the parent keeps catching), that is blocking the parent from feeling emotionally stable enough to deal with baby's upset. (We can see how this could happen at work, in politics, anywhere.)[35]

Here is some more food for thought about how life affects us without our knowing it:

- Social exclusion determines our physiology. For example, people who are socially excluded from a game tend to experience a room as five degrees colder than people who are included in the game.[36]

- The stereotypes we hold determine our capability. Caucasian men who are high math scorers on the SAT, faced with information about how Asians are better than them at math, tend to do much worse on the test than those who don't know about the alleged Asian advantage.[37]

- Our tendency to like things that remind us of ourselves can determine big life choices. For example, a disproportionate number of lawyers' names start with "La" and a disproportionate number of dentists' names start with "Den." A disproportionate number of Louis live in St. Louis. (And this predilection isn't limited to dentists, lawyers, and Louis.)[38]

- Being grouped with someone determines how much we like them. People grouped together in a coin toss quickly prefer the people in their group.[39]

These are all examples of what psychologists call "priming," where something unconscious causes us to behave in a certain way. Our environments are priming us all the time, affecting our perspectives, judgments, affinities, and even our abilities.

This is where just being, and just noticing comes in. We can, through engaging presence, notice how we are feeling, thinking, and behaving in the given circumstances—the context—of the moment we are in.

One way of doing this is by asking ourselves "what?" What is happening right now?

This is what actors spend much of their time doing. Being present to what is happening now. And now. And now. And now. We watch life and see how it is unfolding, by noticing how each moment is a new experience with new information.

If we are the Caucasian men, for example, we can notice that we feel threatened or defensive all of a sudden. If we didn't notice this and didn't allow it to change, if we kept feeling unconsciously threatened or defensive about our math skills, that feeling would eat up our cognitive energy, which in turn, would make us do badly on the math test.

It is not magic how our circumstances impact us. It is logical.

We can also use our imagination in a way that is akin to priming in order to shift our own awareness and increase our possibilities.

For example, right now you can invite yourself to notice your feet. Become present to the soles of your feet and then allow that awareness to spread to the whole of you (presence). Now playfully invite yourself to adopt the thought that "most people are so kind and helpful." Just think those words and notice how you feel. Notice any judgments and then go beyond the judgments to notice what it feels like to hold that thought as true. Imagine that someone walks into the room and you say "hi" to them. How does that interaction go? Notice the soles of your feet again to let that belief go. Now invite yourself to adopt the thought that "most people are such selfish jerks." Notice any judgments and go beyond the judgment and think those words. Notice what it feels like to hold that thought as true. Imagine that someone walks into the room and you say "hi" to them. How does that interaction go? Now let that go by coming back to the soles of your feet again. The thought can drain from the soles of your feet like water out of a bathtub.

Notice which thought felt more familiar. Or did they both feel familiar in different ways?

These different thoughts have underpinnings in different beliefs: people are good, or people are bad. These thoughts and beliefs give rise to different ideals and norms. And different ideals and norms give rise to different actions.

For example, if we think that people are usually jerks and believe that people tend toward badness, then it would be normal and ideal to defend ourselves against other people. The action of defending ourselves then reinforces the idea that we have to defend ourselves, which makes other people seem even more threatening.

If we think that people are helpful and believe that people tend toward goodness, it would be normal and ideal to open ourselves up and connect with other people. The action of opening ourselves reinforces the idea that we can open ourselves, which makes other people seem even less threatening.

If we don't know which way we tend, we'll go around locking our doors or leaving them wide open in every situation without knowing why, and maybe to our detriment.

Every single thing we encounter primes us to feel or think in certain ways. Whether we stop at first appearances is up to us. Sometimes we will. That's fine. Becoming present to our own experience and leaving it at that, is sometimes the right choice. But sometimes we may want to go a step beyond, to see what else lies there waiting to be discovered.

For instance, I started this book with: "We live in a volatile, uncertain, complex, and ambiguous world. Stress... fear... U.S. Army War College."

Notice how reading that makes you feel.

War! Danger! Lurking! Everywhere!

Or:

Danger! Stability. Order. Good.

(And maybe you think: "Yes, I love those things!" or maybe you feel: "Eek! Scary!")

I could have started the book this way instead:

> There is wonder all around us. It is hiding there in the people we meet. It is waiting there in the ideas we encounter. It is resting there in our very own selves. To benefit from the opportunities that are hidden in the nooks and crannies of ourselves, other people, and life, all we need to do is know how to wonder. Luckily, each of us is part of an evolving global community with an exciting opportunity for enrichment thanks to each other's strengths. We can also learn from each other's challenges.

Notice how reading that makes you feel.

Progress. Connection. Potential. Growth.

(And maybe you think: "Yes, I love those things!" or maybe you feel: "Jeezy peezy. Rose-colored glasses. Come on.")

I could have framed it this way:

> Creativity occurs when disparate ideas bounce around and come into contact, bumping up against each other until they are synthesized into something new.

Notice how that feels.

Or this way:

> An athlete studies all possible strategies ahead of time, not just his own. In this way he folds the most helpful strategies into his own playing, and is also ready for any strategy that comes his way. The more strategies he has exposure to, the better he can engage any opponent with nimble intelligence. Similarly, exposure to the varied ways people think, feel, and behave (their conscious, or often unconscious, strategies), allows us to be more flexible, so we can engage any potential business prospect, partner, employee, or employer with more nimble communication.

Notice how that feels.

These are all true. These are all useful ways of looking at the same topic. And each one primes you, orients your mind, differently.

I chose the first, ultimately, because even though the wonder paragraph would prime a cozy, hopeful mood, the creativity paragraph would prime a kind of bouncy optimism, and the athletic paragraph would prime a practical, logical mind-set, the framing I chose more accurately reflects the process suggested in the book: connect with our current reality on a cognitive and emotional level, and then go from there.

Beyond priming, shifting between different framings helps us interrogate our thinking, to "see" in new ways. (There is an exercise for this at the very back of the book that can be done solo or in groups.)

It is helpful for me to be able to choose what frame to use not just to communicate, but to more deeply investigate and understand my own work, and find more creative applications for its use. (True for any business. No?)

So, we can use our ability to be present and flexible this way: to playfully interrupt the immediate circumstances and unconscious influences that take away our agency, so new possibilities can emerge that are more helpful.

What else gets in the way of being grounded and agile?

Expectations About Other People

One tendency that causes us to reject certain ways of thinking, feeling, and being out of hand is that we are always comparing what is happening, to what we think *should* be happening. As we've discussed, we expect other people to behave in certain ways, and when they don't, we don't like it.

Let's say we see a mother with a baby in a stroller, and the baby is crying. We see the mother's down-turned mouth, wrinkled forehead, and tight shoulders. We see her rifling around in the diaper bag. From observing her body, we know the mother is feeling sad and frustrated. We surmise that she is looking for a bottle, a pacifier, or a favorite stuffed animal, some soothing object to help the baby. She takes out a pacifier and gives it to the baby. The baby stops crying. The mother smiles. All is well (maybe).

As we are watching this scene (or even reading it), something is happening to *us* too. Not only are we observing the mother's behavior and the baby's behavior but we are unconsciously internally modeling that behavior as well.[40]

The same motor neurons that are firing to make the mother's fingers rifle through her bag are firing in our brains. If the mother does what we think she should be doing, we feel the same emotional content that the mother is feeling (more intensely if we are highly susceptible to emotional contagion).

We are relieved when the mother finds the pacifier and gives it to the baby, not just because the crying will stop, but because we have lived through the mother's experience with her at a physical level.

But do we always feel complete empathy for a mother with a crying baby? No. We don't. If the mother fails to behave in the ways we expect her to, we don't empathize at all.

We get angry.

We don't just internally simulate what we see. We also match that simulation against previous experiences, norms, and ideals in order to make sure that things are happening as we expect them to.

If what is happening doesn't match what we think should be happening, we feel confused. "Why are they being that way?" We shift from curiosity and empathy to judgment and defensiveness—the catalysts of stress and the death-knells of creativity, empathy, resilience, and choice.

Because childrearing can be a charged subject (in my subjective opinion), let's depart from the harassed mother for a moment and look at playing catch to illustrate this point.

As neuroscientist David Eagleman describes in his book *Incognito: The Secret Lives of The Brain*,[41] if we are playing catch, and I throw the ball to you. You expect it to make an arc and descend either into your hand or onto the ground. You expect this because you have an internal model of physics that has then been reinforced again and again through your exposure to gravity (and may even be hardwired ahead of time).

We are having a nice and easy back and forth game of catch. It is predictable because the ball is behaving the way you expect it to, arcing and falling, arcing and falling. You feel happy. I toss you the ball, but it suddenly vanishes and reappears on your head perfectly balanced. Your internal model does not recognize this way for a ball to behave. You could not have predicted that the ball would do that.

Your brain doesn't have the neural pathways that link together in such a way to make the ball's behavior explainable. At the moment when the expected behavior does not transpire, we get very uncomfortable.

As Eagleman says, it is like we were reading this and, all of a sudden, it turns to पालि, for example.[42] He notes that many of our brains haven't done the cognitive work to be able to read this (Pali) script, so to those brains it doesn't make sense. But it does make sense to those of you who know how to read Pali.[43]

Understanding other people's behaviors can sometimes be like trying to understand another language. (Sometimes even our own behavior can seem this way.) We've all experienced this bafflement.

When this bucking of expected behavior occurs, if we have no tools with which to encounter otherness, we get scared, angry, or paralyzed. We are not interested in understanding *why* the ball acted this way, or what the strange-to-us writing means. We just want things to go back to normal so we can feel safe again.

We know this simply from being humans on the planet. As neuroscientist Robert Sapolsky says: "It shouldn't take neuroscience to 'prove' what we think and feel."[44]

So, let's return to the mother with her crying baby. Why would we get angry with this woman? From the safety of these pages, we can see that she is doing the best she can, based on her own norms.

Why, in the actual moment, might we get so mad?

We get mad for the same reasons we go into fight, flight, or freeze when the ball does what we don't understand.

In fact, our reaction can go beyond not empathizing, to maliciously wanting the mother or ball thrower to suffer for their wrongs.

We can actually feel joy at the pain of people whose behaviors seem foreign to us. Even kindergarteners feel this joy![45] There is a word for this: *schadenfreude*. *Schaden*, damage. *Freude*, joy.

Not only do we get a feel good jolt out of *seeing* wrongdoers punished, but we get a jolt out of punishing people directly for wrongs done, even at our own expense.

In one study people were willing to risk losing a game (all of their money) in order to get the rush of punishing other players for their wrongs.[46] If someone acts in a way we don't like, we will bite off our nose to spite our face and feel good about it, because the act of punishing others for their wrongs makes us feel so good. Through their punishment, our own norms are reinforced, so when strange-to-us behaviors are punished we feel safer.[47]

As we've seen, our norms are norms because they have worked for us. This is why having our norms affirmed, and protecting our norms feels good. Protecting the status quo keeps things stable for us, but gets in the way of our curiosity, ability to connect, and to be creative.

In order to stay open to new ways of being without feeling threatened by them, we can become fluent in ways of being that are different from our own.

But, as we've talked about, we can't just force ourselves to become open to other ways of being. That can feel far too threatening. And, in fact, biologically we can't change how we respond in certain moments.

In a dialogue with the Dalai Lama, psychologist and emotion expert Paul Ekman explains what this means:

> One of the reasons we have so much difficulty once we become emotional is that the emotion itself enslaves us. There is what I call a refractory period, in which new information doesn't enter or, if it does, our interpretation is biased and we only regard the world in a way that supports the emotion we are feeling. That refractory period may be only a few seconds or it may be much longer. As long as it is occurring, we can't get out of the grip of that emotion.[48]

Biologically, a refractory period is the tiny slice of time when a nerve or muscle can't do anything after it has fired.

Psychologically, it is the time when we can't do anything about how we feel. The emotion is responding to a cue, so it can't respond to our attempt to reason ourselves out of feeling, thinking, or acting in a certain way.

But this refractory period lasts only 90 seconds, as neuroscientist Jill Bolte Taylor notes in her book, *My Stroke of Insight*:

> Once triggered, the chemical released by my brain surges through my body and I have a physiological experience. Within 90 seconds from the initial trigger, the chemical component of my anger has completely dissipated from my blood and my automatic response is over. If, however, I remain angry after those 90 seconds have passed, then it is because I have chosen to let that circuit continue to run.[49]

Again, this is why the presence aspect of supermindfulness is so important.

If we can just be with that experience, without trying to change it or do something about it while it is happening, then it can move through us. Released from the refractory period of the emotion, and having experienced the emotion fully, we can then engage curiosity.

We can remain present to see how our experience unfolds, how it changes, and what insights it reveals. We can remain present to notice and really value our own experience, and to see how our own norms and expectations are shaping that experience. We can see what's happening right now, just as it is.

We can ask: what is true for me? What is my experience? What is my version of reality? What is important to me?

In connecting with our own reality, our own experience, and without trying to change ourselves in any way (like people in an acting class are not trying to change themselves), we help ourselves to relax, and from there, we naturally expand out again to see what else there might be to learn when (and if) we are ready.

As billionaire and mindfulness champion Ray Dalio says about running his hedge fund: "Creativity is not coming from 'working the brain' and 'I will work hard and think about it.' It comes from this deep state of relaxation."[50]

Both in relationship to our own experience and to others, we can engage a spirit of playfulness. A sense of "shruggy" wonder. When we are exploring other possibilities we can ask: what else might be true? What if I looked at this experience in another way? What about this way? What about that way?

Again, if we start to feel threatened by playing around with other possibilities, we can become present to that experience, include it, and let go of trying to see in a new way for the moment. Because, in that case, the reality of our discomfort is our current reality. Playfulness is not. Our own experience is as valuable as other possible perspectives, just as other possible perspectives can be as valuable as our own. They are all experiences for us to have and mine for their value.

As father of Organizational Behavior, Ed Schein said: "All experience is data."[51]

And, beyond expectations, we ourselves can be powerful obfuscators of who other people wholly are. We rarely have the chance to see other people as they are with people other than us, so we forget that we are only seeing a few facets of any given person.

I remember hearing my mom on the phone once when I was in my early twenties. She was laughing and open and relaxed. After the call I asked: "Why aren't you like how you were on the phone, with me?" She said: "Because that was my best friend, and I feel really safe and comfortable around her."

"Why don't you feel safe around me?" I asked.

"Because you are kind of mean to me," she said.

"How am I mean to you?" I asked.

She explained that I would often share my opinion about, for example, her clothes. My doing that felt judgmental and mean to her. To me, sharing my thoughts was kind and helpful; it was my way of showing that I care. To her it felt the opposite, and I had no idea. So, it was my own way of expressing care that was actually causing her to close down around me.

Circling back to expectations, when I looked more deeply, I saw that the suggestions I was offering reflected *my* values, *my* aesthetic, *my* idea of what would be fun or satisfying. The reason my "care" felt especially bad to her was that it wasn't being offered in response to who she really was, but who I (apparently) thought she should be.

In another instance of our own selves blocking our ability to see other people, I saw my otherwise quiet, retiring cousin doing a dance move called "the worm" at her wedding, surrounded by her friends. I thought: "I have no idea who this person is."

I realized that, because I had thought she was quiet and retiring, I had spent most of our relationship doing the talking. Because I spent most of our relationship doing the talking, she was quiet and retiring. After seeing the worm performance, I decided to talk less and ask more questions. Lo and behold, whole worlds about her opened up to me, and now we are close, close friends.

And sometimes it is not ourselves at all, but the context in which we meet someone that obfuscates or illuminates aspects of themselves. For example, I was teaching acting to and creating a film with a group of teenage boys who were in a "last chance" program. In the context of creating art, all of these amazing talents and ideas came pouring out of them. They were kind and funny and dedicated and creative. I said: "Does your math teacher know that you can be like this?" They laughed and laughed.

We are different with different people and in different contexts. Psychologist Joshua Aronson calls one facet of this fact Conditional Stupidity, where in relation to certain people, we can't seem to summon our full intelligence. Social discomfort corrodes intellectual coherence.[52]

In portraying a character, actors know that the character changes—slightly or drastically—depending on who they are with or the situation they are in. This is not because the character is dissembling or manipulative. Simply, different contexts draw out different aspects of who and how we are.

We understand people in relation to ourselves, and other people understand us in relation to themselves. We often don't know how we—by being ourselves, or by being in the context in which we are encountering someone—are determining who they seem to be.

Expectations About Ourselves

As we've seen, our expectations of how people should be affects how we respond to them.

Well, we are people too.

We also have expectations about how we should be. Deviating from who we think we are can feel frightening (without playfulness). We have a Self-Concept that puts us into those labeled boxes. We also take short cuts in how we think, feel, and see ourselves too.

Let's see how we might rediscover how to hold our wholeness and mine that complexity for its wealth of wisdom.

First, why don't we?

One way in which we miss out on our own rich, wholeness is in our relationship to our own thinking. We tend to see thoughts as good or bad rather than as helpful and unhelpful. Good and bad are categorical. Helpful and unhelpful are situational. Categorical orientations keep us out of the moment.

If certain thoughts are always deemed to be good, and certain thoughts are always deemed to be bad, when we find ourselves thinking thoughts from the bad category, we feel worry and shame, which create stress. That then amplifies the worrisome thoughts, causing us to experience them even more strongly, and engaging us in a cyclical battle against ourselves, instead of allowing those ways of thinking to spark curiosity in us. We worry about worrying.

Actors don't ask if a character's thoughts are good or bad. They ask why those thoughts are there and what they are trying to accomplish for the character. They allow thoughts to invite inquiry and investigation, to engage them in creative exploration.

We can extend that same courtesy to ourselves. Wouldn't that be kind?

When we pause to notice what we are thinking, we notice—as we saw with feelings when we talked about emotional contagion— that sometimes our thoughts aren't actually constitutional to us, or worthy of deep investigation.

Intrusive Thoughts, for example, are an incredibly common phenomenon where violent or disturbing images pop into the mind, seemingly out of nowhere. As Dr. Timothy Legg attests:

> [T]hese thoughts, however, are just thoughts. They seemingly appear out of nowhere, cause anxiety, but have no meaning in your life. They're not warning messages or red flags. They're simply thoughts. What gives them power is that people who experience them become worried about their significance.[53]

Sometimes the best choice is to, as with emotions (or as an actor exploring a character's thoughts), just let them flow through us with ease and a loose grip. We can step back, watch them go, separate from us, but still curious to us.

Or, we can treat them as we would a character's thoughts. We can ask, why would someone have these thoughts? What would their function be?

We miss out on mining our wholeness by how we tend to treat emotions, as well. We have decided that some feelings *are* good and some *are* bad just because some feelings *feel* good and some *feel* bad.

Actors look, instead, at emotions as information.

Actors learn that emotions are most often the byproduct of needs fulfilled or not fulfilled. They are the byproducts of actions taken or thwarted, not just pesky or nice sensations happening in a vacuum. (And if they *are* a purely chemical phenomena, then that is good information to have, as *that* is their context.)

Emotions are often not ends in themselves. They are responses to something and calls to action.

Emotional Intelligence expert Joshua Freedman of the organization Six Seconds presents how emotions are like little packages of information that inspire appropriate action. Each emotion asks us a question and also motivates us.[54]

He writes:

Fear motivates *protection*.

Anger motivates *attack*.

Joy motivates *connection*.

Disgust motivates *rejection*.

Trust motivates *stepping forward*.

Sorrow motivates *withdrawing*.

Surprise motivates *stopping to assess*.

Anticipation motivates *looking forward*.

There are myriad combinations of these feelings, expressed in thousands of words.

Obviously, there are more than eight emotions (many more, maybe infinite, as emotions are experienced on a spectrum and in relation, always, to the disposition of the person feeling them), and even exactly what constitutes a real emotion is debated, but every emotion (like every other way of being and doing) serves a purpose, which is why we feel them.

And while lovely feeling emotions and good feeling connections increase creativity, productivity, integration, and learning,[55] so-called "negative" emotions exist for a reason as well.

In his book *Personality: What Makes You The Way You Are*, on how genetics give rise to behavior, biological anthropologist Daniel Nettle compares negative emotions to smoke detectors and notes that they "are clearly there for a reason. They are protective systems for our body and mind, and it would be disastrous to lack them entirely."[56]

Allowing painful feelings to spark curiosity can be really difficult, and I am a fellow traveler in creating a new relationship with these feelings.

One friend of mine joked that I have left "no stone unturned in ways to avoid uncomfortable feelings." And that is pretty accurate. But the more we try to avoid certain thoughts or feelings, the more frightening they seem, because in avoiding them we are sending ourselves the message they are, in fact, frightening. The train of thought stops there. Feeling. Ah! Run away.

The more we are able to be present with, and curious about all different ways of feeling, the more nuanced and masterful our relationship with our feelings becomes. When we learn to allow them and listen to them instead of fearing them, feelings can step into their role as information-givers rather than tormentors. Usually, in relationship to any given moment, we are experiencing many different emotions, many textures that have a lot of great information for us.

Being comfortable with lots of ways of feeling is called "emotional diversity" or "emodiversity," and it is linked to overall better wellbeing. A study associated with Harvard Business School surveyed 37,000 people and found a relationship between emotional diversity and both physical and mental health. In their discussion they posited why this might be:

> [E]xperiencing many different specific emotional states (e.g., anger, shame, and sadness) may have more adaptive value than experiencing fewer and/or more global states (e.g. feeling bad), as these specific emotions provide richer information about which behavior in one's repertoire is

more suited for dealing with a given affective situation. Second, reporting a wide variety of emotions might also be a sign of a self-aware and authentic life; such emotional self-awareness and authenticity have been repeatedly linked to health and wellbeing. Finally, an intriguing possibility could be that, as with research suggesting that biodiversity increases resilience to negative events because a single predator cannot wipe out an entire ecosystem, emodiversity may prevent specific emotions—in particular detrimental ones such as acute stress, anger, or sadness—from dominating the emotional ecosystem.[57]

Research into emotional granularity, people's ability to identify more specific and nuanced emotions, indicates that the more granular our understanding of our own feelings, the better our social and emotional intelligence and mental health.[58]

As neuroscientist Lisa Feldman Barrett notes in her book *How Emotions Are Made*:

> In a collection of scientific studies, people who could distinguish finely among their unpleasant feelings—those "50 shades of feeling crappy"—were 30 per cent more flexible when regulating their emotions, less likely to drink excessively when stressed, and less likely to retaliate aggressively against someone who has hurt them.[59]

Again, when actors play a character who is experiencing uncomfortable thoughts and feelings, they become curious about them. They extend curiosity and wonder.

They ask why a character is feeling that way. What is happening? They see that their thoughts and feelings are indicators of something amiss to them, not end points. They see that their feelings evolve and change, sometimes quickly.

We can, through presence, see ourselves from this slight distance as well, while still feeling and thinking fully. From this slight distance we can extend to ourselves the same curiosity and compassion that we freely offer to fictional people.

This doesn't mean that we have to analyze every single thing we feel, only that we have the option of staying present to our experience to see what it has to tell us.

Danger

Again, when we assume that a way of thinking, feeling, or behaving is bad or has no value, we can get no value from it. This doesn't mean that we like every way of being. No! This also doesn't mean that we condone every way of thinking, feeling, or behaving. No! This only means that if we pause to consider a given thought, feeling, or action, then we have the possibility of gaining new insights into it. Instead of only labeling and shaming behavior, we can gain a lot by looking a little longer, and a little more deeply. And with a little more playfulness.

Or, as Harvard psychologist and implicit bias researcher Mahzarin Benaji said: "My favorite word is 'understanding.' I know it's somewhat colder than the word 'compassion' or 'empathy'… I believe that when you understand, you are left with no option but to change in some way."[60]

Some ways of thinking, feeling, and behaving we don't want to understand. We just want them to go away because they are truly threatening and definitely damaging. But running away from understanding does not bring us closer to safety. It does not bring us closer to a solution that really changes the thing we dislike or fear.

As Archbishop Desmond Tutu said: "There comes a point where we need to stop just pulling people out of the river. We need to go upstream and find out why they're falling in."[61]

Going beyond their likes and dislikes, actors interrogate the why of a character's behavior. The more we practice doing this, the more the fear we feel becomes an invitation to understand, rather than retreat. This is not to exonerate the other person, but to free ourselves from our own discomfort.

We can't just do this.

We need a system for doing this. Actors have one. They look at not only the psychological but also the interpersonal and social structures that give rise to what is happening, to try to understand what would cause a person to think, feel, and act the way they do.

This investigation doesn't have anything to do with the rightness or wrongness of the behavior. And it doesn't result in excuses. It is simply a different orientation from the one we usually use when faced with what we dislike (inside or outside ourselves).

Author and community-building activist Theo E.J. Wilson illustrates this so beautifully in his talk *A black man goes undercover with the alt-right,* where he talks about his experience of doing exactly that:

> Never in a billion years did I think that I could have some kind of compassion for people who hated my guts. Now, mind you, not enough compassion like I want to be friends. I don't have infinite olive branches to extend to people who, like, would not want to see me on this planet. Right? But just enough compassion to understand how they got to where they are... The point is that to get to this point of understanding, you have to let go of that fear and embrace your curiosity, and sadly, too many people will not take that journey to see the world from the other side... We have to understand something. Human beings all want the same things and we have to go through each other to get these things. These courageous conversations are the way that

these bridges are built. It's time that we start seeing people as people and not simply the ideas that we project onto them or react to. Human beings are not the barriers but the gateways to the very things that we want. This is a collective and conscious evolution.

Not curiosity, not conversation, but rejection and shame are the tactics we more often use to stop people's behaviors when these behaviors seem like barriers to us.

But the effectiveness of shame as a deterrent depends on the desire of the shamed to be in relation to the shamer. If we don't care about having a connection with someone, we don't care if they reject us. The less connected we are, the less effective shame is. When there is already disconnection, shaming each other drives us further into our defensive corners rather than motivating change.

Employing shame is our cultural tendency to get people to change their behavior, and it tends to work in the short-term but at the cost of trust and connection. And usually people need the opposite of shame in order to change not just their behavior, but their minds.

In fact, research into adult development from Scott Taylor, Associate Professor of Organizational Behavior, shows that it is not forcing people to contend with the worst aspects of themselves that helps people sustain change. It is holding for them and with them the image, not just the possibility but the high probability, that they can be their best selves. Whatever that means to them.[62]

Viktor Frankl, psychologist and holocaust survivor, echoed this finding when he quoted Goethe in a famous lecture saying: "When we treat man as he is we make him worse than he is. When we treat him as if he already was what he potentially could be we make him what he should be."[63]

And in our current line of thought we can see that, when we turn away forever from all curiosity about something, it becomes difficult to respond dynamically to the true needs of the moment in relation to that thing. In fact, we often respond in ways that are counter to achieving our own objectives.

Adding to this thought, we can circle back to Banaji's perspective about understanding and bring in Einstein's voice again when he wrote: "Everything that men do or think concerns the satisfaction of the needs they feel or the escape from pain."[64]

When we look at behavior from this angle, we might see it differently.

Everyone Thinks They Are the Good Guy

Despite how we sometimes view ourselves, we tend to see ourselves as the hero of any situation, and we aren't keen on giving people the benefit of the doubt.

We tend to judge ourselves by how we feel. ("I'm exhausted. That's why my email had a typo.") While we judge others by what they do. ("He is careless. That's why his email had a typo.") One negative action from another person often defines their whole "self" and we leave it at that.

This is how movies work. We never see the point of view of the "bad guy," so we revel in his demise.

But this is the problem: everyone thinks they are the good guy.

Actors are trained to get behind the reason for other people's behaviors so they can play the "good guy" *and* the "bad guy." In this case as well, actors need to understand why someone is doing what they are doing instead of focusing on whether they like the behavior or not.

Whether it's a character or another person, we can dislike them all we want. That alone is not going to change them. We might as well understand why they are doing what they are doing, so we can move forward from the standstill of disdain and learn something too.

How do we do that? How might we help make incomprehensible behavior that we hate, comprehensible and something we can actually grow from, ourselves?

The easiest way is through contrast.

One way to look at conflict is to see it as nothing more than contrasting needs.

We don't usually see other people's actions as an expression of their needs, because we don't have the tools to engage with the viewpoints that give rise to needs that are other than our own.

But, like shadow and light, conflicting needs can reveal each other. They cast each other into relief, exposing one another, which creates greater clarity and the potential for creative synthesis.

What if it is not right versus wrong, or good versus bad that creates conflict? What if it is one need versus another need?

In acting, these are called "conflicting objectives." I am trying to satisfy my objective. You are trying to satisfy your objective. The story is born of these objectives in conflict.

Even more foundational than objectives-at-odds are values-at-odds.

In acting, a term that points to the character's value-structure is called their "super-objective." Values and super-objectives are not exactly the same thing, but playing around with different super-objectives can serve as a helpful way to experience how our values affect how we think, feel, and behave, and also to help us see what values we hold strongly, and which we don't.

A super-objective is the overall driving force that all of a character's objectives are working to achieve. A character's super-objective might be Power. Or Love. Or Peace. Or Justice. If a character's super-objective is Justice then in a given circumstance, his objective (or need) might be to uncover the truth! Whereas if a character's super-objective is Love, given the same circumstance, the love-driven character's objective (or need) might to be to foster connection.

This is true for us as well. We each have overarching values that drive us and determine how we deal with any given moment we encounter.

In life, obviously we have more than one super-objective and more than one value. But our conflicts and greatest befuddlements in understanding one another often come from super-objectives, or values, in conflict. (Sometimes even within our own selves.)

If there is no conflict, there is no story. No story, i.e. lack of conflict, makes for an unhelpful movie or play, because we use movies and plays to help us understand how to deal with social and personal challenges.

In Ancient Greece, all citizens were required to attend the theater because the discussions triggered by the plays helped the viewers co-create their society. Observing and reflecting on conflict together helped them create agreed upon social and personal ideals and norms. It helped them learn to tell the same story; to interpret life in the same way.

Theater, television, movies, and even music are still helpful this way. They create fictions that we can reflect on and draw on, but we rarely have that goal in mind when we are consuming them, and we largely do so some from the isolation of our living rooms or earbuds.

The communal experience of consuming fiction changes the experience because we get immediate, unmediated feedback from the people around us.

I remember one theatrical production of *Macbeth* I saw. It was performed in Japanese with English supertitles. In the most tragic moments (or traditionally-to-me, tragic moments), the people around me who seemed to know Japanese were laughing uproariously. (I am still wondering about why.)

In response to a play I was acting in, *Phaedra's Love*, half of the audience was still laughing in the lobby afterwards. The other half were so angry and disgusted that some were crying.

From the safety of our homes, cars, and earbuds, we will tend to think that how we are receiving a given story is how everyone is receiving it. And our social media echo chambers reverberate this back to us.

But the better we are at coming together to interpret the real and fictional stories that inform and create our lives, the more power we have, as the brilliant historian Yuval Noah Harari proposes:

> Humans control the planet because they are the only animals that can cooperate both flexibly and in very large numbers. Now, there are other animals—like the social insects, the bees, the ants—that can cooperate in large numbers, but they don't do so flexibly... Now suppose I've managed to convince you perhaps that yes, we control the world because we can cooperate flexibly in large numbers. The next question that immediately arises in the mind of an inquisitive listener is: How, exactly, do we do it? What enables us alone, of all the animals, to cooperate in such a way? The answer is our imagination. We can cooperate flexibly with countless numbers of strangers, because we alone, of all the animals on the planet, can create and believe fictions, fictional stories. And as long as everybody believes in the same fiction, everybody obeys and follows the same rules, the same norms, the same values.

And when we can't it's because we don't believe the same fictions, but, because they are fictions … we can imagine what it would feel like to believe something that someone else believes (especially why it benefits them to believe what they believe) in order to understand them while still believing what we believe.[65]

Our ability to directly encounter otherness and to imagine allows us to live, society-build, and innovate better, not in spite of our differences—the contrasting stories and needs that are revealed through conflict—but because of them.

Sometimes a conflict we are experiencing isn't even about what we need, and it isn't due to foundational differences in the stories we are inside of. Two people might have the same need and the same story, but their way of communicating makes it seem as if they are in conflict.

Just the vibe of another person creates the conflicting contrast. In this case, the contrast is in the delivery.

Imagine that you are part of a team at work, and on that team you have someone who tends toward optimism and someone else who tends toward pessimism. (Picture right now what kind of person comes to mind when you hear those two words. Optimist. Pessimist. You can use stereotyping labels to create awareness and spark curiosity for yourself.)

As psychologists describe them, people who tend to be more optimistic have an easy time starting projects because they believe that the process will be smooth, fun, and will work out. However, the inevitable bump in the road is at odds with their expectations, so when they hit a snag they think that they must be on the wrong track, so they give up.

Pessimists, on the other hand, have a harder time starting projects because they assume things will go wrong, but once they begin, they have more perseverance because they expect the bumps, so the setbacks seem like no big deal and they keep going.[66]

They both might have the need or desire to keep the team on track, but the optimist might propose undertaking new ventures to achieve this end, while the pessimist proposes persistence.

But it is easy to see how it would be great to have both kinds of people in a group: one to help get things going, and one to help keep things going.

The problem is that these two kinds of temperaments often have difficulty tolerating each other well, so friction and misunderstandings accompany their helpful differences.

We can see how it would be helpful to harness the beneficial aspects of optimism and pessimism in our own selves as well.

If we are geared toward one way of being, we can see how the occasional practice of the other way of being would help to make it more normal to us, and could be helpful to us.

How can we do that?

One way is through using contrast to fuel our imaginations. Through experiencing opposites, like hard and soft, or rough and smooth, the contrasting qualities reveal each other.

And once we experience something, we have experienced it, so we can use it. Let's try with optimism and pessimism.

In order to get behind what gives rise to the behavior of optimism or pessimism, we can use several different flexibility-building practices.

I like calling the practices that help us access more possibilities, "Momentary Imaginative Immersions,"[67] because this is what neuroscientists call what we do naturally when we mirror people to understand them better. Without even trying to (as we've seen), we momentarily imaginatively immerse ourselves in other ways of being.

In our case, we are making this unconscious process conscious, so we can include and also go beyond our judgments. We are using our ability to observe other people and to imaginatively invent, to not only understand other people better but to experience new ways of being that can serve *us* as well.

(The Momentary Imaginative Immersion practices are described in greater detail on p.110, so feel free to take a look there now if you'd like. But you can also jump right in.)

Momentary Imaginative Immersion: Beliefs

Become present to where you are as you are, by noticing the backs of your shoulders, the backs of your knees, and the soles of your feet, and look about you for a moment. (Presence)

Let's use thoughts to imaginatively immerse ourselves first. Notice what it is like to believe "things work out," "life is easy," "it's no problem." (Just reading those three phrases notice how you feel.) Go ahead and adopt those beliefs as if they are your own. Invite yourself to easily and playfully think: "It's no problem. Things work out. Life is easy." Notice how that feels. What's the benefit? If someone were to come up to you right now as you are thinking this way, how might you greet them? (Possibilities)

Let that go. Come back to where you are as you are, by noticing the backs of your shoulders, the backs of your knees, and the soles of your feet, and by looking about you. (Presence)

Now notice what it's like to believe: "success takes hard work," "things don't always work out," "life is a challenge." (Just reading those three, notice how you feel.) Go ahead and adopt those beliefs as if they are your own. Invite yourself to easily and playfully think: "Success takes hard work. Things don't always work out right away. Life is a challenge." Notice how that feels. What's the benefit? From this perspective, if someone were to come in, how might you greet them? (Possibilities)

Let that go. Come back to where you are as you are, by noticing the backs of your shoulders, the backs of your knees, and the soles of your feet, and by looking about you. (Presence)

Momentary Imaginative Immersion: Disposition

Another way we can practice is through experiencing possible usual dispositions that might give rise to the expression of optimism and pessimism.

One way to evoke the sensation of a disposition is through qualities. Qualities are not good or bad. They are just elemental descriptors.

According to Webster's they just are "the attribute of an elementary sensation that makes it fundamentally unlike any other sensation."

I think of qualities as anyway you would describe something in nature:

Rough, Soft, Hard, Bright, Dark, Spikey, Dull. Bright, Clean, Dusty, Smooth, Flat, Wavy. These kinds of things. They aren't good. They aren't bad. They are all differently useful.

A rough pillowcase wouldn't be very helpful, nor would a soft piece of sandpaper.

So, first, bring your awareness to the back of your neck, to your lower back, and to the backs of your knees. Sense the space behind, and the space around you. (Presence)

Then adopt the quality of Bright. Like a bright, bright light. Notice what the quality of brightness feels like.

Then add to Bright the quality of Open. Like a wide-open space. Notice what this quality of openness feels like with bright.

Then add to Bright and Open the quality of Light. Like a feather floating on the breeze. Notice what this quality of lightness feels like with bright and open.

Brightness. Openness. Lightness. Invite yourself to feel as if you have a bright, open, lightness inside you and all about you. You are bright, open, and light. What if that's how you move through the world? If you were to greet someone when you were experiencing this disposition, what would that look like and feel like? Also, notice any judgments you have of these qualities. Note those judgments, if there are any, and then see what it is like to go beyond the judgments to see what the actual experience of being Bright, Open, and Light is like. How it is helpful to be Bright, Open, and Light? Describe to yourself how it is helpful to be Bright, Open, and Light.

Good. Let that go by bringing your awareness to the back of your neck, to your lower back, and to the backs of your knees. Sense the space behind and the space around you. (Presence)

We can also adopt the usual disposition of pessimists by adopting the qualities of Closed, Sharp, and Heavy.

Invite yourself to adopt a quality of Closed. Like a shut door.

Then add to Closed a quality of Sharp. Like the point of a knife.

Then add to Closed and Sharp the quality of Heavy. Heavy like a bag of rocks.

Go ahead and adopt those qualities, as if you are Closed, Sharp, and Heavy. (And there are lots of kinds of pessimists. Infinite. This is just one.) What if that's how you move through the world: Closed, Sharp, and Heavy? If you were to greet someone when you were experiencing this disposition, what would that look like and feel like? And again, notice any judgments you have of these qualities. Note those judgments, if there are any. Then see what it is like to go beyond the judgments, and to see what the actual experience of being Closed, Sharp, and Heavy is like. How is it helpful to be Closed, Sharp, and Heavy? Describe to yourself how it is helpful to be Closed, Sharp, and Heavy. (Possibilities)

Good. Let that go by bringing your awareness to the back of your neck, to your lower back, and to the backs of your knees. Sense the space behind and around you. (Presence)

One of the ways of being that we played around with above—optimistic or pessimistic—you may not love. That feeling tells you, you don't usually operate that way. (Or it is a way in which you wish you didn't.)

And this is the other helpful thing about contrast. It illuminates what's usual for us and what's unusual, what we like and dislike, so we start to see ourselves more clearly.

Once we experience those ways of seeing—"things work out," "life is easy," "it's no problem," "success takes hard work," "things don't always work out," "life is hard," and Bright, Open, Light, Closed,

Sharp, Heavy—we can draw on them. And when someone else is behaving in accordance with those underlying mind-sets, that person won't seem so odd any more.

Lastly, we can see that those are just aspects of people and of ourselves. There is a big difference between calling someone "an optimist" and describing them as "optimistic."

A frequently light, bright, open person can also think pessimistically (and go darker and more closed than just being pessimistic). People are complex—they aren't only one thing. We are playing with the building blocks of perception, so we can increase our ability to hold this complexity in ourselves and others.

Like any new way of doing something, looking through the lens of an alternate belief or disposition without wanting to make fun of it might not feel easy right away. We are used to mocking differences, both imagined (as in the exercises above), and observed (as in the people we encounter), rather than mining them for insight and creative material. This is one way we mitigate our discomfort with unfamiliar or disliked ways of being and needs that are counter to our own.

Above, we used pure imagination to immerse ourselves in different ways of being. We can also use observation to access new possibilities. When observing someone else, especially someone who is different from us or who makes us feel uncomfortable, the first impulse might be to mock them internally or react strongly against how they are.

One participant during a workshop I was leading said: "I mirror people all the time, usually behind their backs after they've left the room." Other people in the group laughed knowingly. This is how we are used to taking on other people's ways of being: making fun of them. We can do that, certainly.

But, if we'd like to, we can also go beyond that impulse to see what else is there. We can include our dislike while still investigating.

I call actors "ambassadors of empathy" because they want to try to stand in other people's shoes. As Meryl Streep said: "I'm curious about people. That's the essence of my acting. I'm interested in what it would be like to be you."[68] My students and collaborators have inspired me to believe that we can all be ambassadors of empathy once we know how. And again, curious, interested, and empathizing don't mean celebrating, condoning, and liking. They just mean seeing what other peoples' reasons and experiences might be.

And playing around in this way sometimes makes us realize that we are the ones who are unreasonable. In one workshop I was teaching, someone in the group asked if something as small as crossing your arms makes a difference to how we think and feel. So we tried crossing our arms across our chests in different ways—right over left then left over right—to see how and if those felt different. The majority of the group usually crossed in one direction and when we crossed in the other direction they said things like: "Oh I hate that!" "It's so uncomfortable," and "Oh, this is awful. People who cross their arms this way should die."

Then they heard themselves and realized their reactions to an insignificant action like arm crossing were probably a little stronger than they would choose. If they felt this strongly about arm crossing, how might they feel about something that really mattered to them?

And that group with that exercise wasn't an anomaly. I've had similar responses to different exercises from people in groups from business to education to wellness.

And we all have triggers along these same lines: other people breathing through their mouths, or breathing through their noses, or using the word "um" or using the word "like," or swallowing loudly, or drinking or eating loudly, or not making eye contact, or making eye contact, or blowing their nose loudly, or sniffling instead of blowing their nose, or slouching, or sitting too straight, or smiling and laughing a lot, or not smiling or laughing a lot.

We feel strongly about tiny things and that's okay! It's normal. But we can feel strongly and still learn.

Fully listening to ourselves and our true, honest responses to different ways of thinking, feeling, and behaving can be as valuable as actively engaging other possible ways of being. Being fully present to, and honest about, how much we dislike (or love) something, however ridiculous (or vulnerable the feeling), helps us see ourselves more clearly.

Once we have fully heard and valued our honest response ("I hate it when..."), and we feel that we want to go further, then we can play around with new possibilities. We can use the interplay between our experience of mocking or lambasting and our experience of investigating, as an opportunity to notice judgments, biases, preferences, and opinions we didn't know we had, and to practice listening to ourselves. Sometimes we need to be present to our own experience for a period before we are willing to entertain any other perspectives.

This, again, is where the importance of playfulness comes in. Kids on a playground have no problem playing all the parts of the story. They find it fun to play the villain. They find it fun to play the damsel in distress.

We don't have to stop playing because we're adults. We don't have to stop experiencing.

As Judi Dench said: "I'd like to play a villain again... [And] I'm always saying to my agent, 'where's the part where the person learns to walk a tightrope then turns into a dragon in the third act. Where's that part?' "[69]

Or as author J.K. Rowling said:

> Imagination is not only the uniquely human capacity to envision that which is not, and therefore the fount of all invention and innovation. In its arguably most transformative and revelatory capacity, it is the power that enables us to empathize with humans whose experiences we have never shared. Unlike any other creature on this planet, humans can learn and understand, without having experienced. They can think themselves into other people's places... I think the willfully unimaginative see more monsters. They are often more afraid.[70]

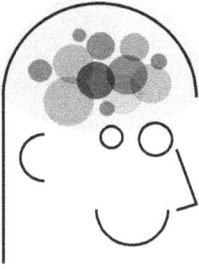

What to Do

Fake It Till You Make It?

Many people, when they encounter this work think: "Great! I can just practice a way of being that I have always wanted to be and then I can change myself forever!" That is true! Maybe.

Yes, these tools are perfectly suited to help us practice new ways of thinking, feeling, and being. But it's helpful to keep a few things in mind before we dive willy-nilly into self-correction.

It is important to note, for example, that when pessimists are asked to think optimistic thoughts while performing a task, they do worse on the task, and when optimists think pessimistic thoughts they do worse.[71]

This means that, in the short-term, launching into the "power of positive thinking" can make people who tend to go negative even more tied up. And launching into "face the facts" can make those who tend to go positive bump their heads against reality pretty harshly.

This is because, in the brain, energy for attention is scarce. When we have no practice thinking or being a certain way, the energy it takes to attend to the new mind-set will compete with the energy needed to perform the task at hand.

In fact, what we can hold in our conscious mind versus our unconscious mind is like the relationship between a Post-it note and NASA's computer system, as psychologist Heidi Grant Halvorson puts it in her book *Succeed: How We Can Reach Our Goals*.[72]

In the short-term, adopting optimism or pessimism competes with the habit at hand. But through playful, imaginative, and observed exposure, we can add more ways of thinking and being to our NASA-sized intuition over time. Relationships and ideas which would never have been likely otherwise, thus become more probable, especially if we play around with different ways of being when the stakes are low.

Walking down the street while playing around with tenderness is much easier than trying to play around with tenderness in the middle of a fight, for example.

Neuroscience also supports the "neurons that fire together, wire together" model of learning that underpins the burgeoning field of neuroplasticity. The more we practice a way of being, the more quickly the neurons connected to that way of being fire for us.

That's true, but it is not all there is to it.

Even beyond the immediate environmental and social conditions we find ourselves in, biologically we aren't a blank slate. Rats born in a laboratory that have never seen a cat get scared when first exposed to the smell of a cat.[73] That makes sense, as the cat is a natural predator.

But fear of the smell of something as innocuous as cherry blossoms can also travel from generation to generation though the DNA of lab rats. If grandparent rats were conditioned to associate the smell of cherry blossoms with pain, grandchildren rats are afraid of the lovely smell.[74] Some studies show epigenetic memories being passed down through 14 generations.[75]

For humans too, genetics and epigenetics (how environment shapes our genetic predispositions) help to determine what we like or don't like, and what we do or don't do, more than we may think, but they don't dominate us completely.

In her book, *The How of Happiness*, social psychologist Sonja Lyubomirsky notes that: "in order to express or not express themselves, genes need a particular environment or a particular behavior."

Our environment is our culture, our family, our peers, our city, etc. and they all influence us greatly without our input or even our knowledge. So, it is only this "particular behavior" piece of our environment that allows us to even potentially direct how we are. We can't determine the particular external environment, but we can give ourselves particular behaviors that help shape how we relate to that environment.

At least in terms of happiness, Lyubomirsky says:

> 50 per cent of individual differences in happiness are governed by genes, 10 per cent by life circumstances, and the remaining 40 by what we *do* and how we *think*... If an unhappy person wants to experience interest, enthusiasm, contentment, peace and joy, he or she can make it happen by learning the habits of a happy person. [76]

So, we have some (40%) choice in a robust dialogue, with genetics (50%), and environment (10%). (You can take this very roughly. Individuals are all different, and science is always learning. The point is we do not have 100% access to huge transformations, nor are we 100% bound to circumstance.)

Daniel Nettle, again, notes that we can't change *who* we are but we can direct *how* we are:

> For example, a high-Extraversion scorer [on psychology's standardized Big Five personality test] who rides around on a motorcycle can rationally decide that it is just too dangerous, and take up some exciting but slightly less hazardous pursuit instead. For every personality characteristic, the set of possible behavioral expressions is very large. People's basic dispositions will surface in some way or other, but they have considerable capacity to decide just which way they will allow it to surface... You don't have to change yourself. You just have to change your outlet.[77]

Or even more optimistically, psychiatrist John Ratey writes in his iconic book *A User's Guide to the Brain: Perception, Attention, and the Four Theaters of the Brain*:

> Changing the brain's firing patterns through repeated thought and action is also what is responsible for the initiation of self-choice, freedom, will, and discipline... We always have the ability to remodel our brains. To change the wiring in one skill, you must engage in some activity that is unfamiliar, novel to you but related to that skill, because simply repeating the same activity only maintains established connections.[78]

So, we *can* change ourselves (at least a little).

However, we aren't always a good judge of what that change should be.

Society's current model of the ideal person tends to sway us quite a lot. By playing characters from different time periods, actors know that different eras had very different ideas of what being a desirable person looked like physically, intellectually, and emotionally, and that most people either aspire to or rebel against the fickle standard of what is ideal in any given era.

If we are naturally good at being a worker bee, but are born into a society that tells us we should all be queen-bee-innovators, we might try to force ourselves to innovate too. But maybe we shouldn't. After all, who will work to turn those new ideas into reality?

And, as a character in a novel by Gore Vidal noted: "But, of course, no one can ever know himself. Nothing human is fully calculable; even to ourselves we are strange."[79]

But, let's say we are fully aware of social influences, we aren't strange to ourselves, and we know what we want to change. Our own desire to change can thwart our ability to change because, usually, we want to change something we don't like. This means we tend to focus on stopping a behavior.

Enter, stage left, the Ironic Processing Theory: "Don't think about chocolate!!!" You are thinking about chocolate now.

"Stop being nervous." Feeling calm?

"Don't slack off!" I bet the last thing you *want* to do is work hard. (Generally, we don't enjoy being yelled at, even by ourselves.)

The Ironic Processing Theory provides the science behind the adage: "whatever we resist persists." In *Making Habits Breaking Habits*, psychologist Jeremy Dean explains what happens when we try to stop a behavior, thought or feeling:

> First, I distract myself by intentionally thinking about something else. Secondly, and here comes the irony, my mind starts an unconscious monitoring process to check if I'm thinking about the thing I'm not supposed to think about. The trouble comes when I consciously stop trying to distract myself and the unconscious process carries on

looking out for the thing I was trying to suppress. Anything it sees that looks vaguely like the target triggers the thought again and round I go in another loop of thinking the same thought I was desperately trying to forget.[80]

We try to distract ourselves from doing something and then, says Dean, we inevitably binge on it when our defenses are down.

In fact, the ways we think, feel, and behave are like rivers that flow in well-worn beds. The water can't be stopped or it will explode in a rush and deepen the bed. If we want the river to change, it has to be diverted to form another bed.

The trick is that it can't know that it is being diverted or it will get vigilant about monitoring whether it is diverting successfully, which keeps it flowing down the same bed or stuck in between the two forks.

Frustrating!

Dean says that the way to shift the river of our neuronal pathways is to focus less on stopping the behavior and focus more on practicing an alternative behavior. When we want to have a cigarette, we chew a stick of gum. When we want to watch TV, we go for a run.

In changing a physical habit there are other important factors like the belief that the habit can be changed, wanting to change the habit, and being in an environment and social group that is conducive to changing the habit. But this book isn't about making or breaking physical habits in particular. This is a book about shifting perspective.

Unlike adopting the habit of exercising or breaking the habit of eating tubs of icing, which are physical, definable, and observable actions, the acts of perceiving—thinking and feeling—are not directly observable.

If someone says "go running" we know what they mean: put one foot in front of the other at a faster pace than walking, for a while. If someone says "let it go" it is less clear from an actionable point of view how to go about "letting it go." Maybe we have not really observed or experienced what "letting it go" looks like or feels like.

Perceptions are learned implicitly from unconscious exposure to other people and our own responses to life. We see our dad get mad every time someone cuts him off while driving, and we learn to perceive that cutting someone off while driving makes people angry. We perceive that cutting off is bad and that the person who does the cutting off is bad.

But as Hamlet said: "There is nothing either good or bad but thinking makes it so."[81]

Another person could have driven with a dad who laughed every time he got cut off, and sped up to try and race the person who cut him off. In this scenario, we might have learned that getting cut off is a funny game.

In the brain, norms are just neural circuits (like the river above) that flow along. Having these norms, in the form of neural circuits, keeps us from getting exhausted. If we were to constantly question every viewpoint we held, we would never get anything done.

In society, norms are what keep social order. It can be dangerous to cut people off, so perceiving the act as "bad" and the person doing it as "bad" with the accompanying feelings of anger and defensiveness to reinforce the fact that it shouldn't happen can help keep us and other people safe.

As we've seen, the difficulty presents itself when our norms, neural and social, actually make us less safe, inhibit our ability to form relationships, or limit our ability to innovate. When this is the case then we want to be able to change our perceptions.

If we are of the danger-is-funny mind-set we might, for example, want to change that mind-set when we have our own kids. If we are of the danger-is-angering mind-set, we might want to change *that* mind-set when we have our own kids, because maybe anger isn't the only response to fear. Maybe we don't need to curse the other person to drive home the message of safe driving. (Or maybe we do. But wouldn't it be nice to choose?)

In the realm of emotions, these learned responses and emotional habits are called emotional scripts. They are written through our exposure to interpersonal, social, and cultural norms interacting with our genetic predispositions, by linking certain cues to certain emotions. Much of this script is written in infancy and is "stored… as rough, wordless blueprints for emotional life,"[82] as Daniel Goleman explains in his landmark book *Emotional Intelligence.*

But, for the most part, predisposition and blueprints don't condemn us to see the world only one way. Whether for emotions, thoughts, or doings, we can write new scripts.

As we've seen, we can experience different emotions, beliefs, and characteristics through engaging our playful imagination. We can shift how we are being, to shift how we are seeing.

But, in daily life, when an internal experience gets linked with an event, person, idea, or type of event, person, or idea, we get stuck because we've coded X means Y, and until we make X mean P, for us, X will mean Y.

Let's take sarcasm, for example. Sarcasm is a form of humor where the person who is supposed to laugh is also the butt of the joke. In a sarcastic exchange intended to be funny, a person is asked to laugh at the expense of themselves. Some people like it. Some people don't.

Whether we laugh, cry, or get defensive depends on our particular emotional script.

Person A Receives a Sarcastic Comment ➜ Feels Happy ➜ Laughs

Person B Receives a Sarcastic Comment ➜ Feels Sad ➜ Cries

Person C Receives a Sarcastic Comment ➜ Feels Mad ➜ Yells

Whether we are Person A, B, or C depends largely on what our exposure has been to other peoples' reactions to sarcasm. If we saw people laugh after a sarcastic comment growing up, our brains developed neural pathways linking sarcasm to happiness. If we saw people withdraw, cry, or become sullen after a sarcastic comment was made, our brains created neural connections between sarcasm and sadness. If we saw someone yell, storm out, or punch the person who made the comment, our brains chemically link sarcasm to anger. Written on our brains is our script of what we have been exposed to, and how we have made sense of that exposure.

In order to rewrite our scripts and shift on this level of thinking and feeling, we have to be exposed to the underpinnings of different behaviors. Not just the behaviors themselves. We have to experience the thoughts and feelings that give rise to the new behaviors: the thoughts and feelings that make those particular behaviors seem like the obvious choice.

That is what the possibilities practice offers. Possibilities help us write new scripts, more scripts. They teach us how to generate new perspectives on purpose, not necessarily so we can be different than we are, but so we can be authentically more of ourselves: so we can have more spontaneous perspectives to choose from in that moment, resulting in more possibilities of actions to take.

As the Ironic Processing Theory reveals, we can't take a negative action. We can't not do something. We have to be (and are always) doing something instead.

The possibilities practice allows us to take positive action and give ourselves the experience of new ways of being, so we can add more scripts, new estuaries to our riverbeds, so the water flows more easily where it needs to go to serve the moment.

The Ironic Processing Theory also makes clear that we can't just jump straight to the desired outcome. We can't just say: "No more anxiety! Joy all the time!" We have to experience the inner state that would give rise to the way we would like to be.

What would the type of the "Joy all the time!" that we are trying to achieve feel like? A soft, fluffy sort of a feeling? A bursting, fast, bright sort of feeling? An open, expansive, embracing sort of feeling? Would the thought "all is well" give rise to our version of joy? Or "awesome! This rocks! Thank you!" Or "I'm amazing!" Or something else? (Remember Stanislavsky's "to know is synonymous with to feel.")

Furthermore, however we would like to be, or have decided ahead of time that we should be, doesn't always serve us. Our natural response is sometimes perfectly developed to give us resilience and agility.

For example, we are all familiar with suggestions like "think positive," "buck up," and "don't let it get you down."

But in a study, *They Stoop to Conquer*,[83] MIT psychologist John Riskind found that slumping after a defeat actually helps us rebound from it faster.

He found that when we feel defeated and we resist slumping—in other words when we resist what we naturally do when we feel "down," which is to physically droop down—we become less resilient than if we do what we feel like doing (slumping), and move on from there. If we physically mask our disappointment, we lose motivation and persist less next time.

On the flip side, he found that if we are told to slump after a win, we also become less motivated. People feel as if they have less control and report that they are more depressed than if they had been allowed to sit in the posture congruent with the circumstance: the upright posture that usually means: "I won!"

So, we see that, in the moment, if we pretend our way out of how we are, we lose out on the intelligence of that way of being.

Through his work, the Australian psychologist Professor Forgas has found that:

> Whereas positive mood [feeling happiness, joy, trust] seems to promote creativity, flexibility, cooperation and reliance on mental shortcuts, negative moods [fear, anger, disgust, sorrow] trigger more attentive, careful thinking, paying greater attention to the external world.[84, 85]

By playing around with and getting more comfortable with these "negative" and "positive" experiences of being a human, we can support our own natural brilliance. Access to diversity of feeling, thought, and action is what makes greater creativity possible. It is not the inner diversity, our whole messy selves, that blocks our creativity. It is our resistance to it.

To circle back to Hamlet's thought: "There is nothing either good or bad but thinking makes it so"—this sentiment seems (and is) in keeping with our theme here, but it is also part of a rather mad scene in the play where several lines later Hamlet admits that he "cannot reason." Hamlet is not necessarily championing this relativistic idea, rather he is exposing, maybe even bemoaning, the lack of order and morality surrounding him. (The world around him was its own kind of VUCA.)

We all need a sense of order to live, both as individuals and in relationships. The invitation to engage curiosity is not so we can welcome a free-for-all, but to create and ignite a true, felt, and lived value system: one that is internally generated and deeply held, and felt, rather than one that is externally imposed that we give lip service to rather than live.

As modern mystic Isha Sadhguru expressed it:

> Once you experience everybody around you as yourself then I don't have to tell you don't kill this person, don't drop that person, don't harm this. All morality will be useless for you because you have experienced everything... The nature of human intelligence is such that, if you don't mess it up with belief systems, every human being will find it. Too many concepts, too many ideas, too many belief systems: human intelligence is corrupt from the beginning. If you do not corrupt human intelligence, just leave it, every human being is capable of knowing this. It is not some superhuman thing. The most important thing to remember is this...is not about becoming superhuman. It is about knowing that being human itself is super.[86]

As the oft quoted sentiment attributed to father of psychology William James goes: "the greatest discovery of my generation is that a man can alter his life by altering his attitudes."[87] If we combine this thought with Sadhguru's then altering our attitude means not just making small tweaks, but revolutionizing how we experience ourselves and each other.

A Taoist parable looks at Hamlet's otherwise hyper-relativistic sentiment of no thing being necessarily good or necessarily bad in another way. And it also speaks to our ability to decide how we might (or might not) want to alter ourselves and our lives.

In the story, a farmer has a son who finds a wild horse and brings it home. The neighbors all say: "How wonderful!"

The farmer says: "Perhaps."

The next day the son falls off the horse and breaks his legs. The neighbors all say: "How horrible."

The farmer says: "Perhaps."

The next day the army comes through to take all of the able-bodied young men off to a fight a war that none of them will come back from. The neighbors all say: "How good for you."

The farmer says: "Perhaps…"

This lens on nothing being good or bad is not from the perspective of morality, but from the perspective of time. We can only see the moment that we are in, so our view is limited.

This story isn't a call to have no feelings about the trials and joys of life. It is a suggestion to stay interested in how one moment links to the next as life unfolds: to stay curious about how different circumstances and parts of ourselves may serve us in ways we don't realize, while also remaining aware that we do have the agency to shift our minds and hearts in order to change.

Presence and Possibilities

Just as there are almost infinite forms of physical exercise, all offering the byproducts of greater strength and greater flexibility for the physical body, so too there are as many types of mindfulness practices offering the same for the inner self. Acting techniques aren't mindfulness practices in the traditional sense, but presence and possibilities have correlatives in the mindfulness field that are helpful and fun to know about.

This is another reason why I call this supermindfulness, because it is not just a dialogue between presence and possibilities, it is also a dialogue between wisdom-traditions, science, and art. So supermindfulness doesn't mean "better than mindfulness." It simply means more than just mindfulness.

The two types of mindfulness practice that acting techniques are related to are those that offer us the ability to be as we are with the moment we are in. (These are presence practices.) And those that offer us the ability to see the moment from different perspectives: to make the familiar strange and the strange familiar, to borrow a phrase. (These are possibility practices.)

Both kinds of practice increase our internal strength and flexibility, so instead of something happening that we don't like and it just wounding or bothering us, we might notice what's happening, notice our response, notice what's helpful about our response, and potentially be curious about what other responses might be helpful, and why. (As I'm sure you've gleaned by now.)

Presence-oriented mindfulness practices were largely brought into the scientific fold by Jon Kabat-Zinn, but have been championed and researched by many others. This kind of mindfulness is simply non-judgmental (or, to frame it as a positive action, curious) observation of one's experience. His actual definition is: "mindfulness is paying attention, in a particular way: on purpose, in the present moment, and non-judgmentally." In one interview he goes on to say: "And then I sometimes add, in the service of self-understanding and wisdom."[88]

In this kind of practice, we notice what is happening internally—physically, mentally, emotionally—without trying to change what is happening, so we can have a clearer picture, a better view. After all, why would we change it when we don't know what it should change to? We only have our one perspective after all.

When we notice our thoughts, feelings, and selves in this accepting, curious, playful way, we begin to see our habits, and we also see that whatever we are experiencing tends to change over time (or quite quickly), like weather patterns. This releases us from feeling so wed to whatever we are experiencing in the moment.

This kind of mindfulness also tends to hook us up to new possibilities automatically. It creates a way of thinking where we notice a reaction or state of being, but we don't try to change it with the same mind-set that gave rise to the reaction or state of being (because, again, what good would that really do?). Instead we watch the nanoseconds to get more information: to see what better impulse or thought we might discover as we follow the path of time with our awareness.

By observing whatever is happening and letting it change by itself, we are often surprised by what it changes to, and by the new insights that arise spontaneously in light of those changes.

Instead of controlling how we are feeling based on how we think we want to feel, we notice how we are actually feeling. We notice that it often changes to a way of feeling that we didn't even know we wanted, or it changes into a way of feeling that brings new insights.

These kinds of mindfulness practices are often done separately from life with eyes closed and distractions at bay, or with a certain goal, as in mindful breathing practices. They are often conflated with, or sometimes synonymous with, meditation practices. These can all be great practices to incorporate into life. These are all ways to practice mindfulness, but this isn't how we will be using them. Instead, our orientation will be with eyes open, inside the flow of life, because our lineage is not mindfulness, it is art.

The other kind of mindfulness is oriented toward possibilities. It is a more creativity provoking kind of mindfulness brought to science by psychologist Ellen Langer. Langer explains mindfulness this way:

> Being mindful is the simple act of drawing novel distinctions. It leads us to greater sensitivity to context and perspective, and ultimately to greater control over our lives. When we engage in mindful learning, we avoid forming mind-sets that unnecessarily limit us.[89]

The possibilities practices in actor training are akin to Langer's work, in spirit. Langer's type of mindfulness involves noticing in a non-judgmental, curious, and playful way what happens when we create a new experience for ourselves that gives rise to a new perspective or outcome.

For example, in one study, Langer had people who didn't like classical music and rap music respectively listen to their disliked genre and find six new things in the music. Not things they liked or didn't like, just six observations. These observations made them like the music better.

In this type of practice, we direct our attention in a more top-down kind of way. In doing this, we notice that where and how we place our attention changes how we experience something. For example, when we ask how something is ugly, we tend to notice its ugliness. When we ask how something is beautiful we tend to notice its beauty.

Langer says: "Mindlessness is the application of yesterday's business solutions to today's problems… And mindfulness is attunement to today's demands to avoid tomorrow's difficulties."[90]

By engaging mindfully with people and ideas in this active, curious way, we gain access to the intelligence and value embedded in a thing we would have missed, by looking at it simply from a "like/ don't like" mind-set.

In several studies of Langer's, this kind of re-perception not only changed perception but also physiology. In a study of hotel chambermaids in New York, one group was informed about the benefits of exercise and asked to name their work as exercise, while a control group continued as they were. After four weeks the group who labeled their bed making, vacuuming, and dusting as exercise lowered their weight, body mass index, blood pressure, and hip to waist ratio.[91]

Both kinds of mindfulness espouse the importance of three orientations, or approaches to learning:[92]

- Non-striving: means that there is no particular outcome that we are trying to achieve, we are simply in the moment we are in, or doing the task that we are doing as we are doing it.

- Inclusive curiosity: means we can invite a sense of curiosity no matter what we are experiencing or encountering.

- Nonattachment: means that instead of seeking to avoid unpleasant experiences (what we have been habituated to dislike), or to retain pleasant experiences (what we have been habituated to like), we can see all experiences as equally valuable. It is happening anyway; we might as well use it for our benefit. Something can be coming at us and we can stand still, shake our heads and say "no, no, no" or we can say: "okay, this is happening... what next?" This doesn't mean that we don't have strong opinions or big feelings about it. Those are included too because those too are happening. Remember, liking and disliking aren't bad. In fact, they are great information! They just might not be the whole story.

Each of these psychological orientations shifts us into a kind of curious "what if" playfulness that mitigates fear, so we can expand and learn.

Both kinds of mindfulness invite us to temporarily soften our grip on the scripts and stories that run through (and rule) our minds, so that new—maybe more helpful—ways of thinking can emerge.

By combining them, we can hone our ability to temporarily suspend our habituated mind-sets, as well as proactively experiencing new mind-sets. When we learn how to experience new ways of thinking, we can access a greater diversity of thought, resulting in greater empathy, choice, and creativity.

Actor training includes both of these genres of mindfulness in an eyes-wide-open, relational way that is also fun, intuitive, and actionable. Actors need to be able to be present, aware, and honest as they are, on a moment to moment basis, *and* they need to be able to immerse themselves in a perspective other than their own.

Actors need to be able to orient themselves toward curiously opening to simply being, so they can hear what the present moment needs. They learn practices that help them do that with more ease. These practices are very much like traditional mindfulness practices but can happen while staying in relationship to the moment that is happening, and the other people in it.

The etymology of "present" is "to be at hand." When we are fully at hand, we are being with whatever is happening as it is happening. We are not fighting with ("I don't want to be feeling that"), fleeing from ("this is uncomfortable. What's happening on Twitter?"), or frozen by our own experience. This allows us to experience ourselves as strong and stable more often, because we are able to be with whatever is happening, more often.

This ability to be fully grounded in life as it is, as it is occurring, is what gives anyone the strength to be curious about, and the stillness to listen for, ways of responding that might be more helpful than our habitual way. Thus, allowing creativity and empathy to flourish.

As we've seen, we live life in patterns of habit. When we feel X, we respond with Y.[93]

For example, as we saw with sarcasm, to one person a joke feels funny and bonding, while to another person that same joke feels cruel and estranging. Neither is wrong necessarily, and neither is right necessarily. Both are differently useful. One response for protecting, and one for connecting.

And anger as a response might be the best choice. Neither kind of mindfulness is about "oming zenly" on a cloud of "Kumbayas," but when we are able to be present with ourselves and with the moment, while being curious about ourselves and the moment, then we are more able to discover the action we really would like to take; a choice we otherwise wouldn't have even known that we didn't have.

We Are All Creators

A survey by IBM of 1,500 executives from 60 countries across 33 industries identified creativity as the #1 business skill for the 21st century.[94]

When we stand in new shoes, look through new eyes, we see things from a new perspective, which we can synthesize with our current perspective to come up with ideas that are truly new, and that can serve more people better.

Pioneering creativity psychologist, Albert Rothenberg, found that the most innovative creativity emerges from synthesizing diverse or opposite perspectives simultaneously held.[95]

He called them Janusian opposites after the god Janus whose faces point in opposite directions with a mind in the middle alchemizing what the two faces experience into something new. The crashing together of different perspectives and worldviews is also why cities incubate innovation so well. Different perspectives sharing tight quarters fosters creativity. By learning how to see our own mindsets and generating new ones inside ourselves, we too can access this alchemic ability.

A survey done by Google on 15 years of data tracking employee success found that, as reported by the *Washington Post*:

> The seven top characteristics of success at Google are all soft skills: being a good coach; communicating and listening well; possessing insights into others (including others different values and points of view); having empathy toward and being supportive of one's colleagues; being a good critical thinker and problem solver; and being able to make connections across complex ideas. Those traits sound more like what one gains as an English or theater major.[96]

One study published in *Science* shows that "reading literature improves... our capacity to identify and understand others' subjective states." [97] If *reading* fiction can do that, just imagine what *being* fiction can do.

These skills are practicable and learnable. We can get better at them, especially if we tackle them through the arts, and acting's tools in particular. It just makes sense to use the discipline that houses creativity and empathy to access creativity and empathy.

And this access to creativity and empathy doesn't only exist on a personal and interpersonal level, but on a social level as well. As we've noted, actors get to mine not just a character's life but a character's whole world.

They gain insight into how everything, from what a person eats, to how the political system they live inside of interacts with how they are, how they construct meaning, and how they make choices. It is a discipline where you don't just get to learn how to stand in someone else's shoes, you get to learn how to stand inside of whole cultures and contexts.

As Google's survey indicates, this is a helpful skill-set to bring outside of imaginary realms and into real life because we need to be able to make connections across complex ideas, think critically, problem solve, support each other, possess insight into ourselves and others, so—from our homes, to our schools, to our places of work, to our planet—we can co-create solutions to the challenges we face that work better for everyone. And this is our responsibility. Each of us.

Our perspectives help create how we construct meaning, which in turn helps determine the actions we take. The actions we take ripple beyond us to help create the social norms that surround us. The social, institutional, and interpersonal facts around us didn't just appear magically. We helped create them or, at the very least, we now live in relationship to them, so by default we are now helping to create what they will become every moment of our lives.

As activist Annie Leonard said in *The Story of Stuff*: "Remember that the old way didn't just happen by itself. It's not like gravity we just gotta live with. People created it. And we're people too. So, let's create something new."[98]

We are all creators. And we are all creative.

We tend to see people as doers of art and consumers of art. The doers are the talented few who are seen to have a monopoly on creativity. "Creative" has been almost completely conflated with "artistic" and "talented." Creativity is seen as an aspect of inherent talent; a character trait rather than a skill.

However, when we were children, we weren't all award-winning artists, but we were all fluent in creativity, and we all naturally used empathy in order to be creative.

We imagined we were villains and heroes and wizards and rulers, and in doing so we explored how to be humans. We watched and mimicked the people in our environment to learn what to do and not to do, think and not to think, feel and not to feel. Through this combination of imagination and observation, we developed our moral code, our beliefs, our understanding of society, and our place in it.

And this was fun. Play.

It was play that we needed for our survival. We had to be able to observationally and imaginatively encounter new ways of being, play around with them, and then integrate what we had experienced back into ourselves in order to understand and interact with our world in a way that helped us succeed.

In this rapidly changing world, our survival depends on our ability to play again, but as adults. We need to gain easy access to this kind of empathic creativity not just so we can respond with creativity and connectedness to other people and to ourselves, but so we can discover innovative solutions that can allow our institutions—our places of work, of prayer, of governance—to work better for everyone.

A viral Twitter meme expresses this well:

> **Every Company**: We'd like to promote mental health in the workplace.

> **Employees**: How about hiring more people so we can feel less pressured and increase our pay so we can keep up with the spiraling cost of living so we're not so stressed out.

> **Every Company**: No not like that. Try yoga.

The goal of awareness and perspective shifting is not to twist ourselves into pretzels to take the shape of warped systems. The goal of awareness and perspective shifting is to allow us to better see the systems that we are inside of, and to provide solutions to make them work better.

Our particular VUCA moment is not calling us to adapt to the ways in which our institutions aren't working, but rather to discover ways in which they can work in new and better ways.

This is a big, important, and exciting responsibility.

By treating both creativity and empathy as skills rather than traits, and by embracing our natural ability to be imaginative, we can liberate all of these ways of being. We can give them back to everyone, and fold them into the natural flow of life, so we can fully step into our roles as the culture creators that we are.

Google and those 1,500 executives identified our ability to empathize and be creative as the most critical skills to acquire, because our world is changing fast and in unexpected ways.

In a globalized world, we can no longer rely on other people's adherence to our own social norms to keep everything stable and static for us—so we can mindlessly go about our business.

In a lot of ways, at home, work, school, and as citizens, we are like children again. We need to be playfully creative in order to navigate the daily challenges being thrown at us, and to use that information wisely and well. Reaching toward empathy is a way to do that.

Supermindfulness in Action

Let's see how we might use the tools we'll be playing with in real life.

One woman I've worked with, who travels a lot for business, uses her ability to imagine proactively by mirroring people at the airport while she walks and waits. She mirrors people to feel and to see what seems to be good and useful about how they go through life. Then she can use what she discovers for herself. It brings meaning to the otherwise transactional, transitory nature of traveling from point A to point B—only in that place at that time are those people she can learn from.

Another woman I worked with found a guy on the sales team of her company to be very aggressive and grating. So, she played around with the qualities he seemed to her to have: bright, fast, large, loud. Some people might call the disposition these qualities give rise to "fun" or "boisterous," but she found them annoying and a bit frightening, because her qualities were more in the vein of small, quiet, and direct. To her, he felt much bigger and louder and wilder than he might have to someone who was louder or faster than she was.

We experience other people in relationship to ourselves. All meaning we make out of another person's way of thinking, feeling, and being is relative to our own ways of thinking, feeling, and being. By playing around with the qualities he seemed to her to have, she noticed that these qualities probably helped him do his job well, and so helped pay her salary. She also noticed that she actually liked some of his qualities. Fast, for example, helped her feel focused, so she could use that.

Another woman I worked with said she was going to bring a "hard" quality into her salary negotiation, because she felt it would give some structure and stability to her naturally softer nature. She felt it would be useful in that context.

I had a profound experience with an acquaintance who is of a different political bent than I am. For years I would hold my tongue and would angrily leave dinners with her. I couldn't believe how judgmental she was. (At least that's why I thought I was angry [it wasn't]. And here I was judging her "judgy-ness"!)

So, for years and years, every time I was with her, I denied my own experience of anger while judging her experience of being judgmental. What can happen from that orientation? Nothing. There is no acceptance that anyone's reality is present—no reality is present.

One night, I decided I needed a new tactic because this other way was too painful. I didn't want to leave that dinner in a fit of rage. I decided to notice how I was feeling as she started to talk. Angry. (Presence)

Then I asked myself what was making me angry. In order to do this I asked: "Why am I angry?" This is a question actors ask continuously about their characters. "Why is a character doing, feeling, saying what they are doing, feeling, and saying?" (Possibilities) Again, we can ask this about ourselves and about other people. In wondering about this, I realized that to me, she sounded angry.

This led me to ask: "What and how?" Actors ask this as well. "How is a character doing, feeling, saying what they are doing, feeling, and saying? In what manner are they doing what they are doing?" (Possibilities) What was she doing and how was she doing it that caused me to perceive her as angry? Then, for the first time, I noticed her tone of voice sounded angry. I thought: "Hmm, maybe I'm just catching her anger." This allowed me to step back from the feeling and create a little distance, so I could still feel the anger but I could also observe it.

I realized that *I* wasn't angry right then. At that moment I was feeling scared and defensive. (I would usually get angry at having felt attacked all night later, in the car.) Why was I scared and defensive? In response to her seemingly angry tone.

So, then I thought, "I wonder what would happen if I listened only to her words." (Possibilities) I decided to ignore her tone of voice and just hear the words she was saying.

In doing that, isolating her words from her tone, I heard *what* she was saying (Presence), and I discovered that she and I share many of the same fears and desires for and about our country. We just have very different ways of addressing them.

Not only did we have a conversation, but one that deepened and created greater nuance in both our ways of thinking. Her angry tone seemed to dissipate, and I wasn't hunkered down in my defensive stance.

Not only that but I was also able to play around with her original tone myself. It was a bold, unwavering, and righteous feeling. It was as if the underlying thought giving rise to her tone of voice was: "if you don't agree with me then you're an idiot." That was different from my usual tone and thought process; another reason it felt uncomfortable and attacking to me. But playing around with her tone as separate from my charged response to it, separate from her, and separate from the content of the conversation, allowed me to access what it feels like to feel so certain and unblinking. She gave me access to those textures of being. Now when I hear that tone, it feels less threatening.

I can also recognize areas of life where I *do* become righteous in this way, and it gives me more awareness and options there too.

I never told her I was doing this. It didn't have to be a big moment of reconciliation. I just stopped for a second to notice more deeply what was happening, to see what else might be possible, mostly because it was too painful not to.

We don't have to wait until it is too painful. We can see people in a new way at any time. And, on some level, we want to move from estrangement to connection.

Humans are social animals. In the most thorough wellbeing study ever conducted, Harvard researchers followed people over 70 years and discovered that the most important ingredient to a sense of wellbeing was robust social connections.[99] (If you think back to Dr. Cloninger's longitudinal study on the three character traits that forecast wellbeing—novelty-seeking, persistence, self-transcendence—you can see how those (developable) traits would give rise to having more robust social connections.)

In places where strong social connections prevail, people live longer and are less likely to be addicted.[100] In fact, loneliness is worse for our health than smoking 15 cigarettes a day,[101] as inflammation increases and the immune system is depressed.[102]

We want to be part of a group. We psychologically want, and biologically need, to be connected to other people, and to the aspects of our own self-concept that help us feel connected to other people, as this reinforces our sense of belonging and safety.

Disconnection from other people causes us physical pain. Studies have shown that feeling rejected by, and estranged from, people causes the same physical pain as being physically hurt.[103] We are hurt when we are disconnected. The more tools we learn to connect, the less pain we feel.

Importantly, when we are observing others in order to access greater connection, we may be wrong in our appraisals of what's going on for them. And that's okay.

It is in the process of trying to understand, that we ignite curiosity, question our assumptions, and expand our possibilities. We are really reaching toward empathy, and in doing that our desire to actually understand someone else grows.

For empathic accuracy, we can ask someone where they are coming from and listen deeply to what they have to say. Exercising the presence aspect of seeing differently helps with our ability to do that: to be there fully and listen. We can learn how to slow ourselves down, opening ourselves to really hearing with our whole selves. That way, we hear where someone else is coming from. In fact, once this kind of thinking becomes more routine, we tend to not want but rather *need* to engage with people in this way.

Part of actor training is also research, and a conversation is nothing more than research.

Imagination and presence spark the curiosity that causes us to desire to know more about where other people are coming from, and to try to find out, so better relationships and outcomes can be had within us and between us. When we feel ourselves to be interconnected in this way, we want to shine the flashlight of our awareness more brightly and with greater precision, because we feel how we benefit from it.

Actors shine their flashlight of awareness on the different aspects of a character they are playing in order to understand them better, and we can do this with anyone. How do they speak? How do they move? What do they say? What do they do? What is their disposition? These combine to express our rich inner lives. Inner lives that are rife with creative material we can use. In this way we can help ourselves to see differently though observation.

We can also adjust the flashlight beam of our awareness to see differently, and to gain access to different textures through pure inventiveness.

For example, what happens to your perspective if your brow is furrowed? Go ahead and slightly furrow your brow and think "life is good." Notice how you can't? Furrowing your brow generates a particular state of being. Or wrinkle your nose and try to think "delicious!" Wrinkling your nose doesn't work.

You could adopt a quality of soft like a down comforter and notice how you feel, and how the world looks through the lens of softness. Or hardness, like you are brick wall. How does the world look through that lens?

As we've seen, greater comfort with a variety of ways of being, and greater awareness of those ways means greater discernment and agency in how we deal with life. We are choosing what we experience anyway, as neuroscientist Sam Harris notes:

> Everything we do is for the purpose of altering consciousness. We form friendships so that we can feel certain emotions, like love, and avoid others, like loneliness. We eat specific foods to enjoy their fleeting presence on our tongues. We read for the pleasure of thinking another person's thoughts.[104]

Actors' tools used in real life are another way to alter our own consciousness for our own benefit.

Or, as mother of improvisation and Second City Founder Viola Spolin said:

> It is highly possible that what is called 'talented behavior' is simply a greater individual capacity for experiencing. From this point of view, it is in the increasing of the individual capacity for experiencing that the untold potentiality of a personality can be evoked.[105]

We can increase our capacity for experiencing in order to discover more in other people and more in ourselves. This stretching can sometimes feel challenging in the short-term, even with playfulness, but so much less difficult than the long-term pain and dysfunction caused by perpetual conflict and estrangement.

Furthermore, while pushing ourselves too far is detrimental, stretching ourselves beyond our comfort zone is what sparks our interest and motivates our vitality, as psychologist and emotional intelligence expert Goleman explains:

> As we move from boredom toward the optimal zone on the performance arc, the brain triggers increasing levels of stress hormones, and we enter the range of "good stress," where our performance picks up. Good stress gets us engaged, enthused and motivated, and mobilizes just enough of the stress hormones cortisol and adrenaline, along with beneficial brain chemicals like dopamine, to do the job effectively. Cortisol and adrenaline have both protective and harmful impacts, and good stress mobilizes their benefits... When demands become too great for us to handle, when the pressure overwhelms us... we enter the zone of bad stress... just beyond the optimal zone at the top of the performance arc, there is a tipping point where the brain secretes too

many stress hormones, and they start to interfere with our ability to work well, to learn, to innovate, to listen, and to plan effectively.[106]

Because we are determining the level of challenge, because we are choosing how far we stretch ourselves in being present and seeing from other people's perspectives, we can find our own sweet spot.

We will know we're out of the sweet spot when we feel too much stress or when we feel bored.

We will know we're in the sweet spot when the world around us seems alive, interesting, and vibrant.

PLAY

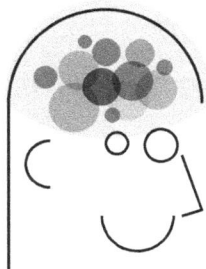

Sparking Wonder: How to Play With Presence and Possibilities to Cultivate Supermindfulness

Momentary Imaginative Immersions

Let's look more closely at how to shine our awareness on different aspects of feeling, thinking and doing in order to momentarily immerse ourselves in other perspectives.

Doing

First, we will look at conditioning our flexibility by shifting physically.

I'll show you how this works.

Momentary Imaginative Immersion

Smile with your eyes and the corners of your mouth and think: "Life is horrible."

Notice how you can't fully? It creates a little cognitive dissonance, or at least a more complex experience than joy or dismay. The smiling eyes and the thought block each other.

Now don't actually smile with your eyes and mouth, just think about smiling with your eyes and mouth. Do you notice how internally modeling that physicality produces the same feeling as actually physically doing it?

Now let your eye corners slightly droop and the corners of your mouth slightly droop. How do you feel? What kinds of thoughts come to you most easily?

Now don't actually droop your eyes or our mouth, just think about drooping them. Do you notice how internally modeling that physicality produces the same feeling as actually physically doing it?

We exist on a spectrum. The fallen expression and the lifted expression reveal each other more fully. We can then notice where on the spectrum we usually lie. We can see that we have access to the whole spectrum, even though it doesn't always feel that way. We can experience the interplay of our bodies, thoughts, and feelings, and how they affect each other. We can see that we have some agency, at least sometimes, in moving along this spectrum. We can identify the granularity that exists along it, the "50 shades of crappy," leading to greater discernment and choice.

Emotions and thoughts don't just affect the body. The body effects emotions and thoughts.[107] Actors know this and use their body's ability to trigger different states of being and ways of thinking.

It's not just the face that can produce different feelings and thoughts. It's every part of the body. And this relationship between the physical, mental, and emotional is universal. Except for certain gestures (like extending the middle finger), how emotions live in the body is unbounded by culture.

This makes sense, because people from different places need to be able to tell if, in general, a person is homicidally angry, or pleased, to avoid being killed and to establish norms, respectively. Subtle differences modulate meaning, but a genuine smile of approval pretty much never means "run for your life."[108, 109, 110]

Most people know that they can identify feelings in other people's bodies, they just don't know that they can also create them in their own.

One way to use the body to shift how we think and feel is by scanning through the face and the body, moving them slightly, and noticing that different ways of holding your body make you think and feel different things.

For example, clenching your fists or relaxing your palms. Bringing your shoulders forward and down versus forward and up. Cocking your chin or tucking your chin. Sitting with your knees spread or your ankles crossed. Exploring different possibilities in this way falls under the invention category, because you are generating different experiences for yourself.

You can also explore possibilities through observation. You can use other people to help you shift (and maybe help you understand them a little better or at least engage with them differently). As we've seen, you can look at another person, slightly take on their physicality, and notice what you notice in how you feel.

As Edgar Allan Poe said:

> When I wish to find out how wise, or how stupid, or how good, or how wicked is any one, or what are his thoughts at the moment, I fashion the expression of my face, as accurately as possible, in accordance with the expression of his, and then wait to see what thoughts or sentiments arise in my mind or heart, as if to match or correspond with the expression.[111]

Of course, Poe's sentiment here comes from where we might be coming from: judgment. We are used to looking at people and asking: good or bad? Like them or don't like them? And that is good. We don't have to like everything, or have everyone like the same things.

However, if we take Poe's suggestion, but also look just beyond our judgments, we may notice that what we call wicked or stupid might be anything but. After all, a wicked person does not necessarily think they are wicked.

Momentary Imaginative Immersion

Look around you right now and choose one person to observe, or if you are alone, think of someone. Now very subtly take on their physicality. How are their shoulders? How are their legs when they are standing? How is their face set? What are their hands doing? Notice what you notice. What does it give you access to that you don't usually have access to?

The next time you are at a café or on the subway, you can take on the postures, or even aspects of the postures, of different people around you.

In this way you can provide yourself with a little creativity break.

You can walk down the street and do this same thing.

Anywhere that other people are (even in your thoughts) is an opportunity to tap into your brain's desire for novelty and play, and in turn, increase your flexibility.

Thinking

We can also shift perspective through invention and observation by using our thoughts, especially our beliefs.

A belief is a synthesis of evidence we have collected.

If we have been exposed to trustworthy people, we are more likely to believe people are trustworthy. If we haven't met such people, then we believe people aren't trustworthy. If I have and you haven't and we both meet someone new and I say, "he's trustworthy," you will have a harder time believing me than if you had also been exposed to trustworthy people. I will also have a hard time understanding your lack of trust.

If I have never seen a green sky, and you tell me "the sky was green," I will have a hard time believing you without seeing it for myself. But if I have seen the aurora borealis and you say "the sky was green," I will have a much easier time believing you.

As we've seen, like our physical habits, our beliefs are largely unconscious. But we can make them conscious through contrast, not just by contrasting them with other people's beliefs, but simply contrasting them inside ourselves.

Momentary Imaginative Immersion

Go ahead and invite yourself to adopt each thought as if it is your own:

"Other people are capable." How does it feel to know that people are usually capable? How does your body feel when you know that people are usually capable? How does the world seem to you? Is this a familiar feeling or unfamiliar feeling? What is the benefit?

"Other people are incompetent." How does it feel to know that people are not usually competent? How does your body feel when you know that people are not usually competent? How does the world seem to you? Is this a familiar feeling or unfamiliar feeling? What is the benefit?

"I am capable." How does it feel to know that you are capable? How does your body feel when you know that you are capable? How does the world seem to you? Is this a familiar feeling or unfamiliar feeling? What is the benefit?

"I am incompetent." How does it feel to know that you are not particularly capable? How does your body feel when you know that you are not very capable? How does the world seem to you? Is this a familiar feeling or unfamiliar feeling? What is the benefit?

"The world is orderly." How does it feel to know that life is orderly and makes sense? How does your body feel when you know that? How does the world seem to you? Is this a familiar feeling or unfamiliar feeling? What is the benefit?

"The world is chaotic." How does it feel to know that life is chaotic and random? How does your body feel when you know that? How does the world seem to you? Is this a familiar feeling or unfamiliar feeling? What is the benefit?

Notice how every way of thinking has some benefit and some cost. It gives you something and deprives you of something.

"People are capable" may cause you to trust someone untrustworthy.

"The world is orderly" may cause you to be rigid.

All blanket beliefs deprive us of discernment. (Even that one.)

For example, we can experience an alternate thought process to the one suggested in this book through adopting certain thoughts as if they were our own (and maybe this is your usual bent, and that's great, as we'll see!):

"We've gotten too weak in our thinking about other people. I don't care about your intentions. I don't care about your context. Your actions are what matter. Just get it together!"

If you adopt this mind-set, you will probably feel a rush of power: there is something motivating and energizing about this disposition.

As Marcel Duchamp encouraged: "I have forced myself to contradict myself, in order to avoid conforming to my own taste."

Duchamp's plan is a good one, because every way of being has a cost.

The take-everyone's-perspective-in-order-to-expand-your-possibilities cost may be that sometimes, in the short-term, we might feel as if we have less clarity and decisive power than we felt a second ago, when adopting the pull-yourself-up-by-your-bootstraps mind-set. It slows us down and sometimes that is not the best choice. Sometimes decisive action is what is called for.

That second mind-set's cost is that it silos us and robs us of learning and connection.

But regardless, both mind-sets are helpful when looked at not as absolutes, creeds, or dogmas, but as tools. One allows us to open. The other to close. One allows us to declare. The other to question. One allows us to connect. The other to command.

There are other mind-sets that are seemingly counter to the one proposed in this book.

"Just ignore what you don't like."

"What other people do is none of my business."

All helpful mind-sets! Just not for every situation. (Sometimes ignoring what we don't like puts us at risk. Sometimes it's helpful to think about and learn from what other people are doing.)

Usually, we have to make a choice about which cost we are willing to pay in order to experience the world, but we don't have to. We can experience a mind-set of powerful, motivating, self-righteousness, and of thoughtful curiosity; of live and let live, and interested engagement. All are helpful at different moments, and all shed different lights that together illuminate the issue more fully.

Feeling

Last, we can shift our perspective through our disposition. Our disposition is our general temperament, our general vibe.

Being able to be aware of and play with our disposition is helpful because people work, live, and create together most efficiently when they have similar dispositions.

People get along better with those who not just think but also feel like they do. Organizational psychologists have found again and again how profoundly disposition affects workplace dynamics and effectiveness. Boisterous people work better with boisterous people. Quiet people with quiet people.[112]

And, psychology aside, we know this from being humans in the world. Guileless, sweet people don't tend to feel most comfortable around cuttingly sarcastic people. People who love to complain and people who love expressing gratitude annoy each other like crazy.

We tend to gravitate toward people who feel like we do.

This is not to say that it is advisable to pretend to feel differently than we do in order to connect with more people. We are who and how we are. And that's wonderful.

Nothing is worth rupturing our integrity. As Alexander Technique teacher Frank Pierce Jones writes in his book *Freedom to Change*: "No matter how many specific ends you may gain you are worse off than before… if in the process of gaining them you destroy the integrity of the organism."[113]

It's just to say that we can play around with different possible ways of feeling, so the dispositions of others don't seem so tortuously strange. Also, along the way we may find that we like some of the other ways of feeling that we discover.

After all, we are not one thing.

As poet Walt Whitman wrote: "Do I contradict myself? Very well. I contradict myself. I am large. I contain multitudes."[114] Again, cultivating supermindfulness doesn't strive to make us different from ourselves, but more of ourselves.

To this end, let's consider a seeming contradiction to Jones' suggestion that we must not destroy the integrity of the organism if we are to flourish.

Harvard Graduate School of Education professor Kurt Fischer suggests:

> To flourish, living systems must be more than just organized. They must be dynamic. Systems must constantly move and change if they are to carry out their functions and maintain their integrity and their interrelations with other functioning systems. A system that becomes static—unable to change and adapt to varying conditions—will quickly perish.[115]

Because we don't live in a vacuum but in dynamic relationships with other people and ourselves, in order to maintain our integrity we actually need to be able to change, and sometimes drastically.

So, we need to have integrity, have a form that is stable, *and* we need to be dynamic and adaptable.

This type of seeming conflict, as David Dinwoodie of The Center for Creative Leadership notes, is not a problem but a polarity:

> A polarity is a pair of interdependent opposites—if you focus on one of those to the neglect or exclusion of the other, at some point in time you dip into negative unintended consequences... Think of it like breathing. Breathing isn't a choice between inhaling or exhaling. If you inhale to the exclusion of exhaling, the negative results show up quickly. And the reverse is also true. The polarity approach says, we must both inhale and exhale."[116]

Authenticity *and* adaptability.

Form *and* fluidity.

The more we expand to include more of our humanity and the more we play around with shifting from one pole to another, the more fluidly we can breathe integrity into the moments of our lives as they dynamically call for our responses.

One way we can expand to include more of our humanity, while feeling more deeply into ourselves as we are, is through shifting into different dispositions.

Momentary Imaginative Immersion

Let's say, for example, we adopt the quality of Brightness like bright, bright light. (You don't even have to move your body, though you can if you like.) Invite yourself to adopt a quality of Bright and notice how you feel when you are bright. Notice any judgments about bright and then go beyond the judgments to momentarily experience this quality of Brightness like bright, bright light. Notice the place you are sitting or standing from this quality of Brightness. If someone were to wave to you, how would you wave back with this quality of Brightness? Notice what kinds of thoughts you have. Notice how having this quality of Brightness is helpful.

Now go back to normal. If it's challenging to go back to normal, engage a presence tool and notice the soles of your feet, then while noticing them on the ground also notice the crown of your head, and then notice your whole self in between. Breathe with your whole self and look around you.

Now invite yourself to adopt a quality of Darkness like a dark, dark night. Invite yourself to adopt a quality of Darkness and notice how you feel when you are dark. Notice any judgments you have about this quality of Darkness, then momentarily go beyond the judgments to experience this quality of deep Darkness. Notice the room from this quality of Dark. If someone were to wave to you, how would you wave back with this quality of Dark? Notice what kinds of thoughts you have. Notice how having this quality of Dark is helpful.

Notice which one feels more familiar to you (if one does).

Come back to just how you are. Feel the ground under you. Look around.

We don't usually allow these kinds of words to be neutral evokers of experience. Usually we use them to define how we feel about someone instead of using them to try to understand them better. We use qualities—rough, bright, open—and characteristics—jerk, sweet, lazy—to describe people.

But a "sweet" person doesn't necessarily see themselves as sweet. A "jerk" doesn't see themselves as a jerk. Their disposition—their felt experience of life—causes them to behave in such a way that other people deem them sweet or a jerk. Sweet and and jerky aren't experiences. They are judgments of other people that emerge when we see their behavior—behavior that is the byproduct of their inner experience.

To play a character deeply, an actor can't just "be sweet" or "be mean," but an actor (and anyone) *can* conjure the internal life that would result in what would be called a sweet or mean disposition by someone else.

Momentary Imaginative Immersion

Invite yourself to adopt the three qualities of Bright (like a light), Sharp (like a knife), and Hard (like a brick). Go ahead and invite yourself to adopt those qualities: Bright, Sharp, and Hard. How do you feel? What if you were to greet someone? How would you greet them?

You probably feel quite powerful and direct. Can you see, however, how someone else might label you as a jerk, or as cold? They might experience you that way, but you don't feel that way. You feel confident and assertive.

Let that go.

Or if you adopt the qualities of Soft, Open, and Bright. Go ahead and adopt the qualities of Soft (like a cloud), Open (like French doors), and Bright (like a candle). Notice what that feels like. Soft, Open, and Bright. How do you feel? What if you were to greet someone? How would you greet them?

You probably feel kind of pleasant and welcoming. Do you see how someone else might label you as sweet, but you don't necessarily feel sweet? At the very least you wouldn't call yourself sweet.

Let that go.

By adopting new qualities, we can shift from *labeling* behavior to *experiencing* the potential experience and intention behind behavior. We shift from just experiencing behavior as it feels to us, by going one crucial step further to include how it *might* feel to someone else, so we can expand our ability to connect, and our own range of being.

That's really all we are doing. We are increasing the ingredients that we have to cook our life experience with; increasing the colors we have to paint our life with; giving ourselves more notes and chords with which to compose our existence, or with which our intuition can compose our existence.

More Presence or More Possibilities?

Just as certain meditative practices can be applied to a particular moment of life to help us achieve goals (deep breathing to regulate emotions, for example), imagination and presence can be applied to situations and creative processes directly to shift our experience on purpose. But it is also helpful to think of them as conditioning our inner strength and flexibility.

To come back to our athlete metaphor, we are social and emotional athletes in this VUCA world.

Both through playing the game itself and through training off the field, athletes condition their physical bodies to be strong and flexible so they are able and ready to respond well to the moments of the game. Conditioning our psycho-emotional bodies through awareness and imagination does the same for the moments of our lives.

We need both. The ability to be strongly grounded in the present moment, deeply honoring our experience, rooted like the roots of a tree into our own ground. And the ability to be flexible and agile, able to see the moment in new ways, like a branch that sways with the breeze. Then, as we go through our lives, we are more frequently, just easily and naturally rooted and flexible without having to think about being rooted and flexible.

As civil rights leader, philosopher, and theologian Howard Thurman wrote:

> We have an established center out of which we can... relate to other men.

And:

> [A] community [and self] cannot feed for long on itself: it can only flourish where always the boundaries are giving way to others from beyond them... Men all belong to each other, and he who shuts himself away diminishes himself. And he who shuts away another from him destroys himself.[117]

Both are true. Both are necessary.

It is likely, however, that your comfort zone lies more toward residing in your own center or more toward boundaries giving way.

It is helpful to discover if you naturally tend toward presence or more toward possibilities because, in all likelihood, if you tend toward one, the other will be less familiar and so you may (or may not) encounter some resistance there.

So, are you more: "Change and grow all the time!" Or "I am as I am"? Here is how you can know which kind of orientation you tend toward.

Imagine this scenario:

You are driving after work in traffic. You're tired and a little cranky. Someone cuts you off. Imagine that happening. What's your first thought?

Is your first thought in the ballpark of: "Learn to drive!" or is your first thought in the realm of: "What's going on there?"? (One is not better than the other.)

If your first thought is judging them ("Learn to drive!") you are probably good at seeing things from your own perspective and knowing how you feel. Bravo! That is wonderful. You may find the presence exercises more familiar and the possibility exercises kind of new.

If your first thought is explaining their behavior ("What's going on there?") then you are probably good at seeing things from other people's perspectives. Bravo! That is wonderful. You may find the possibilities exercises more familiar and the presence exercises to be kind of new… and we know how much our brains like new things we didn't choose. Don't be surprised if there is some resistance to your nondominant way of being.

I am more of a perspective-taker and I hated (I can't stress this enough) just noticing my own experience as it was (being present) for a long time. Being asked to just be there noticing what was happening, was an exercise in torture for me.

However, other people, science, spiritual practices, and artistic disciplines prize presence. As a teacher, I facilitated presence practices (even though I didn't like them) because I was teaching an array of tools from a field of study, not just what worked for me. And some of my students only wanted to do those, and only those, as much as possible.

So (being the diligent perspective-taker that I am) I thought: "Well, there must be something in this presence business beyond torture." So, I kept practicing different ways of being present.

And slowly over time, it dawned on me that I hated it because I was trying to use presence to experience a new perspective. I thought there was some state of being I was supposed to be experiencing through being present. I was convinced there was some "right" way to feel while being mindful. (Something like a monk enshrouded with clouds on a mountain, smiling at a bird perched on my knee while a hurricane raged, and the world around me burned.)

It was only when I started practicing being present from its own actual perspective, that I experienced its benefits. It's not a trick. There's no goal. It's really just saying: "Notice what's happening now. And now. And now."

That's it.

Revelation. Poof. Torture gone.

I didn't have to feel like an aloof enlightened being; I was being invited to notice what was actually happening as it was happening.

Similarly, those who are more of the "I am what I am" persuasion might feel that taking on another perspective feels a bit threatening. And yes! It feels like a threat if you are operating from the mind-set of "I am what I am." In fact, from that mind-set, it *is* a threat. Here you are being who you are, how you are, and someone's coming along and suggesting that you try a different way of being? "No thank you! What's wrong with how I am already?" (You might think.)

So, if you are more of an "I am what I am" person, it might be helpful if you think of taking on new perspectives as being research. (Which it is.)

You really don't have to agree with a new perspective. Judgment and discernment are as important as open-mindedness and curiosity. You can just remind yourself that: "The more extensive a decision maker's experience, the more patterns he or she will be familiar with; the more patterns, the better the intuition." You aren't doing this to change you. You are doing this to "get more data." You will remain intact. You will simply have more knowledge to draw on.

And it's just play. And we've seen playfulness is an important part of learning. We forget this as adults. When we are engaging with the world in this playful way of noticing, and asking: "what is?" "what if?" "what else?" wonder permeates life when we extend our humanity and our curiosity outwards from a strong, centered identity.

There is something new to notice right now.

Something is happening that is worthy of noticing inside or outside you.

Some new way of thinking, feeling, or being to play around with is always available in the form of other people, ideas, the physical world, and your own imagination.

What used to be avoided can become a kernel of new understanding and interest. From this mind-set, we run away less and start being where we are more, because being where we are is an interesting act that feels engaging.

We dissemble less and invite our wholeness and the wholeness of others more often, and easily.

We have more agency to engage with life as it unfolds in front of us.

We discover that we are more creative, empathic, and innovative than we thought.

We can embrace and revel in the differences and seeming paradoxes of life, because we know that from their interplay new ideas are born.

Creative leaders from all arenas echo this chorus.

Artist Max Ernst offers: "Creativity is that marvelous capacity to grasp mutually distinct realities and draw a spark from their juxtaposition."[118]

Author Chimamanda Ngozi Adichie adds: "The single story creates stereotypes, and the problem with stereotypes is not that they are untrue, but that they are incomplete. They make one story become the only story."[119]

And finally, Ancient Roman philosopher and playwright, Terence:[120] *Homo sum, humani nihil a me alienum puto.* (I am human, and nothing of that which is human is alien to me.)

We are human.

We have the ability to go beyond ourselves to become more of ourselves, to connect more fully to other people, and to synthesize "mutually distinct realities" into something wholly new.

The more materials we have to create with, the more we can create.

It's that simple.

The world around us can be a catalyst for creative inspiration anytime, anywhere, if we know how to see it that way.

So, go ahead and shrug your shoulders quickly and think: "I don't know. We'll just see." Now smile slightly. Notice how doing those three tiny actions (shrugging, thinking "I don't know. We'll see," and smiling) make you feel. And let's play!

52 Ways to Wonder: Presence and Possibilities Practices for Cultivating Supermindfulness Anytime, Anywhere

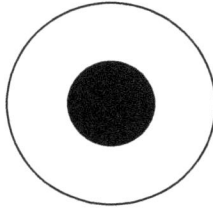

The practices in this book are fun prompts to open you up and spark curiosity. If one feels like it closes you down, you can keep playing with it, or just notice that it closes you down and count *that* as the experience the practice sparked (because it is), and then become curious about it and play with that. Or leave it. Play around with other ones and come back to the one you didn't like another day, month, or year. It's all for fun. If it's not fun, don't worry about it.

You can read one prompt each morning and play around with it throughout your day. Or choose one to notice for the week. (There are 52, so it can be a year-long adventure.)

You can also set a timer to chime once an hour and, just for a moment, connect with the practice you are playing around with that day, or week, or month.

If any of your explorations inspire you to ask a person who sparks your curiosity where they are coming from, or how they are experiencing life, you can try that out too. Curiosity and imagination are stepping stones.

You can also get in touch more deeply with the moment you are in by simply asking:

- What am I willing to wonder about in this moment?

- What am I willing to notice more deeply, more fully?

- Am I willing to wonder about my own experience?

- Am I willing to wonder about someone else's experience?

- Am I willing to wonder about another way of seeing this moment?

Listen to and follow what you hear.

In all presence there are possibilities, and in all possibilities there is presence, and to wonder is a verb.

Have fun!

Others: Presence

Today just periodically become present to the person in front of you. Notice your thoughts and feelings about them. Let those be there. And then go beyond that to just seeing, hearing, and sensing them as they are right then.

Objectives: Presence

Every person has goals they are trying to achieve and actions they are trying to take to achieve those goals. Our behavior reflects our objectives. See what it is like to understand people's behaviors (your own and others') from this point of view today.

- What might be the objective in this moment? What might be their goal in this moment? What might be their need in this moment?

- What particular actions or tactics are being used to achieve the objective?

- Try noticing what they seem to need and how they seem to go about meeting their needs.

Walk: Presence

Just notice how other people move physically through the world. Notice the different ways that people walk, sit, enter and exit rooms, etc. Notice how they strike you, and what they cause you to feel, and think about the person. Just become present to how you experience other people though their movements.

Walk: Possibilities

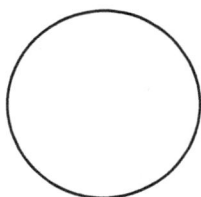

At some point today find someone and adopt their walk. Very subtly take on that person's way of walking and notice how moving like them changes how you feel, think, and see the world.

- How do their feet strike the ground? How do their knees swing? How do their hips and shoulders move? What are their arms and hands doing? How is their head positioned? Do what they are doing.

- What does it feel like to move through the world like they do? What kinds of thoughts and feelings do you have when you are moving this way?

- What are your thoughts about them (likes/dislikes/jealousies/judgments)? You will have like/dislike/better than/worse than/safe/unsafe thoughts about them. That's great. Notice that. Then see how it is to go back to focusing on walking like them again.

- How does what they are doing work for them? How might it be useful to you?

- Notice what you notice.

When you want to come back to yourself just invite yourself to let that other person's walk go and bring your awareness to the soles of your feet, and notice your own walk.

Voice: Presence

Just notice the sounds of voices today. Notice how different voices feel to listen to. Become present to how you experience other people through sound.

- What feels pleasant? What feels unpleasant? Why?

- What assumptions do you notice that you make based on the voice?

- Notice what you notice.

Voice: Possibilities

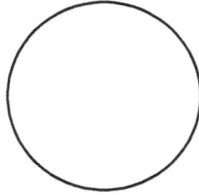

Discover peoples' voices to notice today. Very subtly try out talking like them (even in your own mind) and see what it's like. Notice how talking like someone changes how you feel, think, and see the world. To let that go, come back to your own voice and notice it.

- How loudly do they tend to speak? And where do they speak from? Does the voice come from deep in the body? From the face? From their nose? Is it low or high?

- Do they speak rapidly? Or slowly? Smoothly or haltingly?

- How do they seem to usually end their sentences? With periods? Question marks? Exclamation points? Trailing off?

- What inter-phrases do they use? Like? Um? Hmm? Laughter? Something else?

- How do you feel and how does the world look to you when you are speaking like them (even in your imagination)? What do you have access to that you don't usually have access to?

Style: Possibilities

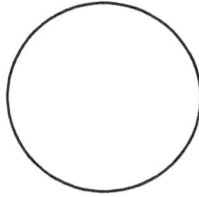

See whose clothes you notice today. Imagine that you had chosen to dress that way. Why would it feel good to dress that way? How do you feel, think, and act if this is how you choose to dress? Take that on and notice what you notice. To let that go, notice what you are wearing, how you feel in it, and how it expresses you.

- Imagine wearing these clothes as clothes you had chosen yourself, how do you sit, stand, and walk?

- How do you interact with other people?

- How do you feel about yourself? What seems important to you?

- Presence: what ideas do you have about the person based on their clothes? How do their clothes seem to express themselves in the rest of the person's personality?

Disposition: Possibilities

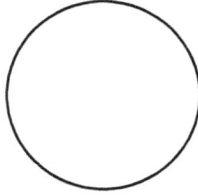

Today notice someone else's disposition and adopt it as your own. Very subtly take on their vibe and see what it's like to live in that feeling state. How does it affect how you feel, think, and see the world? When you want to let that go, invite yourself to let it go and then notice your own current disposition.

- If it is helpful you can name it with qualities like open or closed, fast, fluttering, or slow, steady, wobbly? These aren't judgments. They are sensations and textures. Or if it's not helpful to name them, then don't. You can simply feel the tone of being they seem to go around in and take that on.

- What does it feel like to see the world from this tone of being? Are they having any particular emotion? How does that emotion feel to you from this perspective? Does it feel different from when you have that emotion?

- If they aren't having any emotion that you can discern, you can imagine them having one and see how that feels.

- How would you interact with other people from this state of being? What does it give you access to that you don't usually have?

Stance: Possibilities

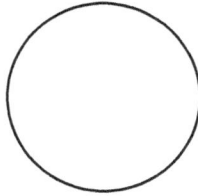

Today notice someone who is relatively still, standing or sitting, and slightly mirror them. Look around from that perspective. Imagine greeting someone. Notice what you notice in your thoughts and feelings when you take on their stance. To let it go, shift a little bit and relax into your own stance.

- How does the world around you seem to you?

- What kinds of thoughts do you have?

- What kind of best friend might you have?

- How might you move through the world?

- How does it make you want to interact with other people?

Soles: Presence

Today just periodically bring your awareness to the soles of your feet as you go about your day. While talking to someone. While writing an email. While eating. While walking. Just include the soles of your feet in your awareness and notice how that affects your experience.

Why: Presence

Today, from time to time, become present to the why of what you are doing.

Ask yourself periodically: "Why am I doing what I am doing right now?"

For any given action there are sometimes several layers of why.

And notice what information you get and how the act of asking affects your experience.

Why: Possibilities

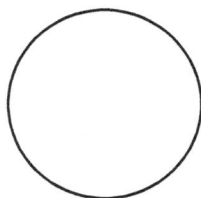

Today, from time to time, become curious about why someone else is doing or saying what they are doing or saying. Play around with the reasons you discover, as if they are your own. How does it feel to have that motivation, to be coming from that place?

How: Presence

From time to time today, notice how you are doing what you are doing. (Is it aggressive? Passive? Slow? Fast? Clenched? Loose?) If you are getting dressed, is it quickly? Luxuriously? If you are washing dishes, are you going fast or slow? Attending or thinking? How does it feel to be doing whatever you are doing in that way? What does it communicate back to yourself or to other people?

How: Possibilities

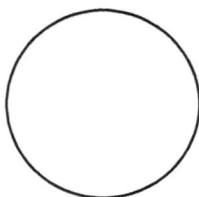

From time to time today, notice how someone else is doing what they are doing. Try it out internally (or physically) yourself. If they are typing on their phone, are they hunched over or leaning back? If they are talking to someone, are they gesturing in a large way, for example? If they are putting on a coat, are they doing it quickly or slowly? How would it feel to do that task that way? How would it feel to approach that situation that way? You can always come back to noticing the soles of your feet or your breath to let go of trying out what they are doing in the way they seem to be doing it in your imagination.

Like New: Presence

Today choose someone you know very well and just consider them as if they are new to you.

- How do they walk?

- How do they talk?

- How do they joke?

- How do they feel?

- What do they seem to care about?

- How do they try to satisfy their objectives?

Thoughts: Presence

Today occasionally notice your thoughts. Include your mental life in your awareness as you do whatever you are doing at that moment. Notice what you notice. Do the thoughts change? Do they repeat? Watch them like a bystander and notice. You can always come back to noticing the soles of your feet or your breath.

Ways to play:

- Periodically listen to the words you say and see what thoughts are driving those words.

- Periodically step back from the traffic of your mind and watch the thoughts go by.

- Periodically choose something to focus on and watch the thoughts that emerge as inspired by that thing.

Emotions: Presence

Today periodically notice your emotional life. Bring the sensations occurring and the emotions they indicate into your awareness while you are doing whatever you are doing. Do they change? Are they stuck? Or fast? Something else? Just watch them like a bystander and notice. You can always come back to noticing the soles of your feet or your breath to stop noticing.

Some ways to play:

- You can notice them as sensations in the body. Where are they in the body? How do they feel as physical sensations? Periodically ask: what emotional sensations do I feel? And notice what you notice.

- You can notice them as weather patterns. Does it feel stormy? Still? Sunny? Cloudy? Periodically ask: what emotional weather patterns do I feel? And notice what you notice.

- You can notice them as images. Maybe you'll notice a clenched fist in your chest. Or a fluttering bird in your stomach. Or a bright light in your head. Periodically bring your attention to some part of the body and notice what images arise when you rest your attention there. If none, then move to another part of the body. Or if you feel an emotion, ask what kind of image it is.

Qualities: Possibilities

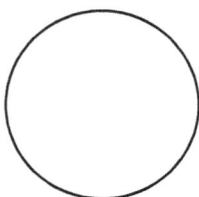

Today let's play around with the qualities of Light and Heavy. In this moment you can invite yourself to adopt a quality of lightness, as if you are filled with feathers or air. Notice what this quality of lightness feels like. How does the world around you seem from this quality of being light? Let that go by noticing your feet and then noticing what quality you have most prominently at this moment, just as you are. Then you can adopt the quality of heaviness, as if you are filled with stones. Notice what that feels like. How does the world around you seem from this quality of being heavy? Then let that go by noticing your own natural quality. Today play around with two qualities to adopt. You can use heavy and light, or qualities from the glossary, or your own. Notice what you notice.

When adopting these qualities:

- What kinds of feelings you have?

- What kinds of thoughts do you have?

- How does the world around you look?

- How do you feel about it?

- How would you interact with other people from this quality?

- When you notice either of these qualities outside you, how do you experience them?

- How about in relationship to each other? You can notice how light looks to heavy and how heavy looks to light, for example.

Conflicting Objectives: Possibilities

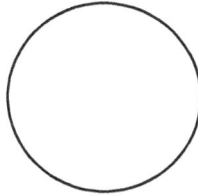

What if it isn't right versus wrong, or good versus bad (though right, wrong, good and bad may be true) that creates conflict? What if it is one need versus another need?

I am trying to satisfy my objective. You are trying to satisfy your objective.

Notice today what happens when you see dynamics through this lens of competing objectives rather than just right or wrong.

We Desire Connection: Possibilities

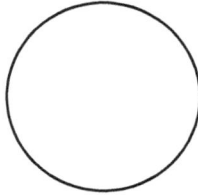

Today play around with noticing how other people's behavior may be their attempt to connect with someone, some group (or even some part of themselves). Today look at other people's behavior through the lens of their desire for being part of a larger group. When encountering someone, ask yourself: "who are they trying to connect with, and how?" And notice what you notice.

Core and Masking Qualities: Possibilities

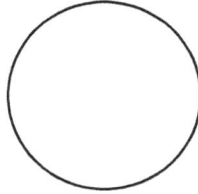

Invite a core quality of Softness. It is as if the core of your being has this quality of softness. Feel what this softness feels like. Keep that, and then mask that softness with a quality of Hard. Like there is a shell of hardness around the core of softness. Notice what that feels like. A soft core masked by hardness. Look around from this perspective. Then let that go by watching yourself breathe in and out a few times and letting it drain out or evaporate, or whatever image or action works best for you. Then invite yourself to imagine that you have a hard core. The core of your being has a hardness about it. A hard quality. Now surround that hardness with a shell of softness. Hard masked by soft. Notice what that feels like. A soft core masked by hard. Look around from this perspective. Then let that go by watching yourself breathe in and out a few times. Today play around with core and masking qualities, these or different ones, and see if you notice them in the world around you.

- Why might you have those core and masking qualities?

- What do they give you?

- How might they cause you to relate to other people?

- How do they cause you to think and feel about yourself?

- What kind of actions might you tend to take from these mind-sets?

Conflicting Qualities: Possibilities

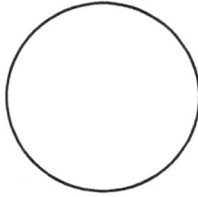

Let's invite the quality of Open. Feel this quality of openness. Imagine saying hello to someone from this quality of openness. Imagine the person's response to you. And now add to Open the quality of Closed. Feel what it's like to be open and closed at the same time (or it might feel as if they are alternating rapidly). Imagine saying hello to someone from these qualities of open and closed. Notice how that would go. Notice how you feel. Imagine the other person's response to you. Look around from this open and closed state. Then let that go by inhaling a deep, clean breath, exhaling both qualities and imagining yourself connecting with someone you love. Today play around with two qualities at the same time, these or different ones.

- How does giving them different amounts of weight change the experience?

- Notice how they aren't mutually exclusive. Do they cause inner tension? What might cause this inner tension?

- What might be the benefit of this inner tension?

- What might your decision-making process be like from this mind-set?

Psychological Actions: Possibilities

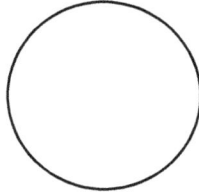

Today let's play around with psychological actions. Let's try on blaming and apologizing. Internally adopt the action of blaming, as if blaming is a frequent thing you do. You are a blamer. Notice how that feels. What benefit does it have? What does it give you access to? Notice the world around you from that state of blaming. Let that go, by breathing it out with your exhale. Then adopt the action of apologizing, as if apologizing is a frequent thing you do. You are an apologizer. Notice the things around you from that state of apologizing. Then let that go by breathing it out on an exhale. Notice what, if any, action is naturally there in you. Just play around with psychological actions today using these, or those from the glossary, or ones you make up.

- Notice any judgments you have about them and completely value those judgments then, for the sake of exploration, go past them momentarily when you are playing around with these actions.

- How do they affect your body?

- How do they affect your mood?

- How would they affect your interactions?

Beliefs About Self: Possibilities

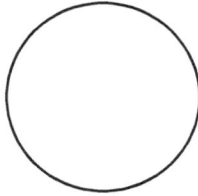

For a moment, invite yourself to be someone who fully believes "I'm capable." Notice how it feels to have that as a deep knowing. Now let that go, by smiling and shrugging and looking at the world around you. For a moment, invite yourself to be someone who fully believes "I'm not very capable." Notice how it feels to have that as a deep knowing that you are not very capable. Now let that go, by smiling and shrugging and looking at the world around you. Play around with adopting beliefs about self as bedrocks today, and notice what you notice in yourself and in other people. (There are more in the glossary.)

- Notice any judgments of either belief and fully embrace them, then go beyond them for a moment to experience what the belief itself generates.

- What benefit do they each have?

- What cost do they each have?

- How do you experience other people from them?

- How would you relate to them?

Beliefs About Others: Possibilities

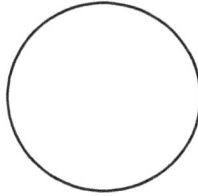

Invite yourself to adopt the belief that "people are great." Notice what that belief of "people are great" feels like. Look around from that perspective. Let that go, by feeling the backs of your shoulders. Now invite yourself to adopt "people are jerks." Notice what the belief of "people are jerks" feels like. Look around from that perspective. Let that go, by feeling the soles of your feet connecting to the ground. Today play around with adopting beliefs about others. Use the glossary or any that you'd like, and notice what you notice in yourself and in the people you encounter.

- How does each belief make you see the environment around you?

- How is each belief helpful?

- How might the beliefs affect what choices you make?

- How might those beliefs affect how you communicate?

Beliefs About the World: Possibilities

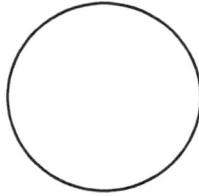

Let's adopt the belief that "life is random." Notice how that feels. "Life is random. What happens is luck and chance." Notice how you relate to the world around you from that mind-set, by looking up and noticing how you feel. Let that go, by feeling your breath and exhaling the thought. Now adopt the belief that "life is orderly and sensible." Notice how that feels. "The things that happen make total sense." Notice how you relate to the world around you from that mind-set by looking up and noticing how you feel. Let that go by feeling your breath and exhaling the thought. Play around with beliefs about the world today and notice what you notice in yourself and in other people. (Use these, or there are more in the glossary, or feel free to create your own.)

- How might these mind-sets affect your choices and actions?

- How might they determine how you relate to other people?

- How do they color how you think about particular events?

- How are they differently helpful and unhelpful?

Core and Masking Beliefs: Possibilities

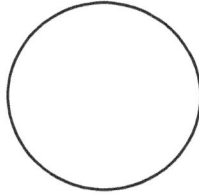

Invite yourself to place the belief of "I'm attractive" at the center or core of your being. Feel how that feels. "I'm attractive." But let's pretend that you don't want anyone to know that you think that, so you wrap that core in the thought "I'm not very attractive." So, you have the core belief of "I'm attractive" with a masking belief of "I'm not very attractive." Notice how that feels. Now flip them, placing "I'm not very attractive" as your core belief. Place "I'm not very attractive" in the core of your being. Feel that to be your truth. And then mask it with "I'm attractive." Notice how that feels. Let that go, by feeling your feet on the ground and softening your jaw. Play around today with adopting and noticing these core and masking beliefs, or use those in the glossary.

- Why might you have either of those internal set ups?

- What do they give you?

- How might they cause you to relate to other people?

- How do they cause you to think and feel about yourself?

- What kind of actions might you tend to take from these mind-sets?

Multiple Beliefs: Possibilities

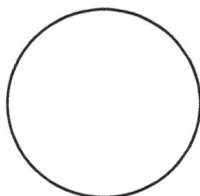

Let's see what it feels like to have two beliefs at the same time. Go ahead and adopt the thought: "I like other people! They are interesting, and I like to learn from and about them." Feel how that feels. Imagine yourself saying hello to someone from this state of being. How does that go? How does that feel? And now add to that thought: "Other people are a little frightening." Feel how that feels. With this new belief added, imagine saying hi to the same person. How does that go? How does that feel? Let that go, by feeling your feet, and then imagining yourself saying hello to someone from your own state of being. Today just play around with two different beliefs. Notice if you see them in action in the world around you too.

- How does giving them different amounts of weight change the experience? What if you mostly feel that other people are frightening, for example? Or mostly feel that they are interesting?

- Notice how they aren't mutually exclusive—they merely cause inner tension.

- What might resolve this inner tension?

- What might cause this inner tension?

- What might be the benefit of this inner tension?

Physical Habits: Possibilities

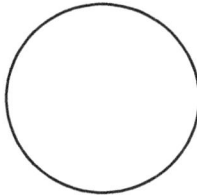

Go ahead and slightly lift your shoulders up to your ears. Notice how that feels. Go beyond uncomfortable or comfortable and notice how it feels emotionally. Now let them drop and slightly puff out your chest. Again, noting comfortable/uncomfortable physically, and going beyond that to notice the emotional feeling evoked. Today let's play around with subtly adopting physical habits like these. You can use shoulders lifted or chest puffed, or choose from the glossary, or make up your own. You can choose one to play with or two to create contrast.

- What happens when you shift physically in one way as you read or write something?

- What happens when you shift physically in the other way as you read or write on the same topic?

- If you play around with each as you walk, notice how it changes your experience of the walk.

- How might you respond to someone you don't agree with when seeing through either of these lenses?

Thought Habits: Possibilities

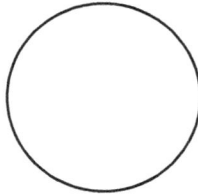

Go ahead and invite yourself to adopt the thought "Is it going to be okay?" Notice how that causes you to feel. "Is it going to be okay?" Imagine that this is a recurring thought habit. Now let that go, by smiling with your mouth and eyes and looking around you. And adopt the thought habit "It's all good." Notice how that causes you to feel. "It's all good." Imagine that this is a recurring thought habit. Let that go, by smiling with your mouth and eyes and looking around you. Play around with thought habits today. Notice what it's like to adopt them at different times so they become the lens through which you see the world. Also notice where these thoughts show up in the world around you.

- Which thought habit is more familiar? Is the way you experience it usually the only way there is to experience it?

- How might you experience other people from these different perspectives?

- How might these perspectives inform the choices you make?

- When you encounter these ways of being in other people, how do you respond? What if you are adopting one or the other? How does that change how you feel about them?

Super-Objectives: Possibilities

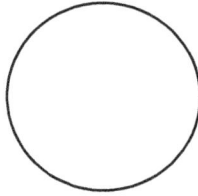

Invite yourself to adopt the super-objective "To win." Your goal is always to win. Notice how it feels to have that goal. In every situation, your desire is to win. Bring someone to mind and imagine greeting them from this objective. How does having the objective of winning make you see and treat the people around you? Let that go, by bringing your awareness to your chest, the whole mask of your face, and the fronts of your legs. Then include the backs of your legs, your back, and the back of your head. Inhale and exhale. Let that go. Now invite yourself to adopt the objective "To be liked." Your goal is always to be liked. Notice how it feels to have that goal. In every situation your desire is to be liked. Bring the same person to mind and imagine greeting them from this objective. How does this objective make you see and treat the people around you? Let that go, by bringing your awareness to your chest, the mask of your face, and the fronts of your legs. Then include the backs of your legs, your back, and the back of your head. Inhale and exhale. Today let's play around with adopting and noticing objectives. Use these, or those in the glossary.

- What is the benefit of each objective?

- What is the cost?

- Notice what surprises arise in playing around and noticing.

- Notice any judgments you have about either one and take that into account. Then go past the judgment to notice the objective.

- How might each objective affect how you approach any given task you have to do today?

Inner Actions: Possibilities

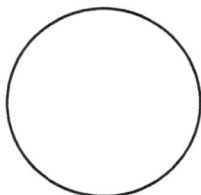

We can use actions to shift our disposition. Right now invite yourself to adopt the inner action of "skipping," as if you are internally skipping. Notice what it feels like to have a light, buoyant sense of skipping. How might you go about your day if your main inner action were to skip? How might you interact with other people? Now let that go, by feeling the soles of the feet, and invite yourself to have the inner action of soaring, as if you are soaring along. Notice what it feels to soar in the breeze. How might you go about your day if your main inner action were to soar? How might you interact with other people? Today play around with these actions, or choose any two actions to play with and notice what you notice.

Lovely/Ugly: Presence

Today periodically adopt the thought "how beautiful" and then notice three ways in which that is true about wherever you are. Then adopt the thought "how ugly" and notice three ways in which that is true about the same location.

Habit: Presence

Today notice one physical habit you have (running your hand through your hair, playing with your cuticles, sighing, cracking your knuckles, touching your face. Things like that). Notice how it feels to do it. Notice what need it serves. Become curious about one physical habit that you notice you do.

PLAY

In-Grouping: Possibilities

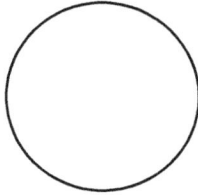

We prefer people we are grouped together with. People grouped together randomly by coin toss tend to quickly and strongly prefer the people in their group.[121] Today notice how you feel toward people you feel similar to, and people you feel different from. Notice the feelings and thoughts you have in relation to different groups of people.

- What would it be like if you were grouped with them?

- How might you be grouped with them?

- How does your experience of them change if you consider them as part of your group?

Textures: Presence

Pay attention to the textures you encounter throughout the day: plants and grass, tree bark, steel buildings, concrete sidewalks, wooden tables, wool sweaters, silk boxers, whatever. Just notice them and if you like/dislike them. What do the textures feel like to you as you encounter them? What is the purpose of a given texture? (People, events, and moods can have textures too.)

Stereotyping: Presence

Children as young as kindergarten stereotype names as being associated with different abilities (Mike = sports. Percival = reading.)[122] Today just notice the images of people that are conjured by their names.

Meaning: Presence

Notice today the meanings you make from the information you receive about other people. For example, maybe someone is in debt. What does that mean about them, to you? Maybe someone is wealthy. What does that mean about them, to you? Or from a certain place? Or educated in a certain way? Or of a certain gender? Or with a certain accent? Or eating a certain food… What if you made a different meaning out of the information? What might that change in how you see, feel, and think about and respond to the person or situation?

Expectations: Presence

As you walk or drive or interact, notice what things you or other people do that make you upset, and what things put you at ease. The things other people do that put you at ease are happening in alignment with what you think they should do. The things other people do that make you upset are things you think they shouldn't be doing.

Today when you feel that upset feeling ask: "What expectation are they not meeting?" Then ask: "What belief underlies the expectation I have?" (i.e. why do I believe that they should be meeting that expectation? Why do I think that expectation is important to meet?)

When you feel that good feeling ask: "What expectations are they meeting?" And: "What belief underlies that expectation?" (i.e. what are they doing that is meeting my expectations? Why do I believe that expectation is important to meet?)

Natural Things: Presence

Today periodically notice the natural things around you (trees, grass, leaves, flowers, glass, wood, metal, etc). Include them in your awareness from time to time, and notice what you notice about how they cause you to feel and think.

Atmospheres: Possibilities

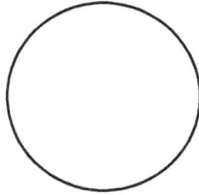

Inner atmospheres are kind of like qualities. We describe people this way: "Easy like Sunday morning," for example. So today we will play around with adopting inner atmospheres. For example, imagine that you have the inner atmosphere of a soft, warm, spring day periodically as you walk around, as if there is a soft, spring day inside you. When you do that, how does the world seem to you? How do you interact with people? What do you feel like doing? What does it give you access to? What kind of intelligence does that way of being have? Notice other people with this atmosphere. Now, imagine that you have the inner atmosphere of a bleak, grey, winter day periodically as you walk around, as if there is a grey, bleak, winter day inside you. When you do that, how does the world seem to you? How do you interact with people? What do you feel like doing? What does it give you access to? What kind of intelligence does that way of being have? Notice other people with that atmosphere. Play back and forth today between soft, warm, spring day, and bleak, grey, winter.

If you just want to adopt one that is fine too.

There are more in the glossary.

Human-Made Things: Presence

Today periodically notice the human-made things around you (cars, houses, roads, buildings, plates, computers, etc). Include them in your awareness from time to time, and notice what you notice about how they cause you to feel and think.

Radius of Influence: Possibilities

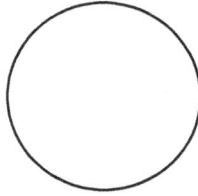

Let's play around with how much space you take up.

First, take up only the size of your chair or where you are standing, as if you have a circle, sphere, or cylinder around you, and you are taking up only that amount of space. Only take up the space that is the size of you. Notice how that feels, notice your breath, notice how much power you feel you have. Then expand that space out to two feet in every direction. How does that feel? Notice what you notice. Then expand the circle out to six feet in every direction: in front of you, behind you, to the sides of you, above you. How does that feel? Notice your breath, notice how much power you feel you have. Then expand to take up the whole room. You fill up and have dominion over the whole thing: every wall, every corner—the whole room. Notice how that feels, notice your breath, notice how much power you feel you have. Then let the radius, the circle, the sphere of influence you have come back to the size most comfortable for you. Notice that. Today notice what happens if periodically you change the amount of space you take up throughout the day.

Radius of Influence: Presence

Right now, just notice how much of the room you feel as if you are taking up, commanding, influencing. A little bit? About half? All of it? More than the room? Today in different situations, notice how much space you are taking up and what causes it to grow or shrink.

Deferring: Presence

Notice how you engage with others when walking or driving. Do you tend to move aside and let a person pass? Or, do you not? Does it matter how the person looks? Does their attractiveness/wealth/ perceived burden matter? Notice what you normally do.

Attribution Error: Presence

Remembering this idea: "We tend to judge ourselves by how we feel ("I'm exhausted. That's why my email had a typo"), while we judge others by what they do. ("He is careless. That's why his email had a typo.") One negative action from another person often defines their whole self, and we leave it at that. In psychology this is called "attribution error."

Today notice where you might not be seeing the whole of someone, and where someone might not be seeing the whole of you.

Notice what noticing that does.

Everyone Is the Hero of Their Own Story: Possibilities

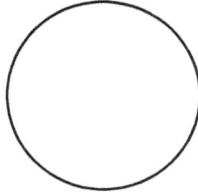

Today notice what happens if you think of everyone as being the hero of their own story. What if everyone thinks what they are saying or doing is right or, at least, necessary in some way?

Status: Presence

Today notice status in your dynamics. In any given situation:

Who has higher status?

Who has lower status?

Is this fixed?

Does it shift?

What does that dynamic feel like?

What does it do?

Status: Possibilities

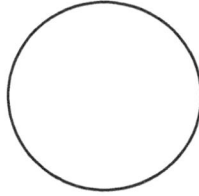

Play around with shifting your status with the people in your life, in your mind.

How might you interact with them differently if your statuses were reversed?

Would any aspect of that be helpful to bring into the actual relationship?

Moment Before and Given Circumstances: Presence

Actors learn that there is always a moment before the scene starts that informs how the scene is played. Are they coming from having a fight with someone? Are they just waking up? Are they hungry and didn't have time to have lunch? Become present today to the moment that came before the moment that you are in periodically, and see how that moment is playing out now. Also take that into account for other people. They have moments before too.

Beyond the moment before, there are the circumstances of life (the ongoing facts of a person's life). Play around with becoming present to how you are experiencing the circumstances of your life. Take other people's circumstances into account too, and notice what you notice.

Self-Concept: Possibilities

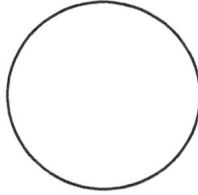

We picture ourselves in a certain way and have particular ways we are trying to be in order to satisfy that image. Deviating from that way can feel scary. So, we are often acting out of a desire to keep stable our relationship with how we see ourselves.

Someone might think: "I am a hard worker," or "I am super laid-back," or "I am compassionate," or "I am a straight talker," or "I am a winner," or "I am a loser."

If you try on these mind-sets, you will see how they have beneficial aspects and damaging aspects. There are intelligent ways of being that keep the person safe, and unintelligent ways of being that undermine the person's wellbeing.

We can play around with different Self-Concepts to open up our own possibilities and see more easily where other people may be coming from. Choose one (or two for contrast) of these today to play around with or make up your own.

Music: Possibilities

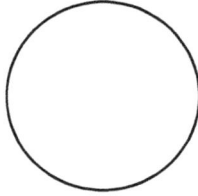

Choose a radio or streaming station and, whatever song comes on, keep doing whatever you are doing but imagine that song is your internal soundtrack or inner atmosphere. What does it feel like if that song is your personality? What does it feel like emotionally? What kinds of thoughts do you have when you are that song? Does it make you move differently? What are the benefits? What does it give you access to that you don't usually have access to?

Then choose another station and let the soundtrack change—embody that song.

Do this with unfamiliar music, from classical, to rap, to country, to BBC news, to pop, to jazz. Notice how having different internal soundtracks changes your mood, thoughts, and lens.

Applied Wonder: Using Wonder to Innovate

The previous techniques are used to deepen, strengthen, and broaden intuition. You do them and allow them to work on you instead of you working on them. But you can also use these practices to access different ways of looking at an issue on purpose as a brainstorming tool.

This can be done by yourself or in a group. It can be done on issues large and small, from the personal, to the social, and the organizational.

But in keeping with the focus of this book, I am just going to focus on how you can use it anytime, anywhere to access your own Janusian creativity.

First, choose the issue or topic you want greater clarity or a new perspective on.

Then, become present to your current experience as it is, allowing it. If it is helpful, you can write it down. Get emotionally granular and specific and validate your own experience fully. No need to push it away. Whatever you resist, persists. So really give yourself the gift of embracing your present experience as it is. Be as frustrated, mad, sad, afraid, happy, excited, or all of those things as you are. Become fully present to your full, messy experience of the topic.

Then, when you feel fully grounded in the reality of what you are experiencing, ask yourself if you are willing to wonder about another way of seeing the issue.

If your answer is: "No, I am not willing to see this from a new perspective," then keep remaining fully and compassionately present to your own experience. Presence has just as much to teach us as possibilities.

If your answer is: "Yes, I am willing to see this from a new perspective," then choose your possibilities tool (Qualities, Beliefs, Super-Objectives, Internal Soundtrack, etc).

Generate three different perspectives from that tool (for example, if you chose Beliefs you might choose to see through the perspectives of "people are jerks," "people are kind," and "I am brilliant"). Then, seeing through each lens, write in a stream of consciousness way. Don't take your pen off the paper until you are done with a given perspective.

At the end of the exercise, you will have your original perspective plus three new perspectives to alchemize into something new.

Here is an example of applying wonder in this way that I did quickly in the car while my daughter was napping. I say that to free you from feeling as if you need to be precious about it. It is an "anywhere" kind of thing you can do to quickly to get unstuck and get your creativity flowing.

I chose as my topic the issue of a colleague not getting back to me about an important task and used Qualities as the tool. How the Qualities I chose caused me to think may be different from how they would cause you to think, and that is totally fine.

These tools interface with each of us as we are. There is no right way to experience imagination.

First, presence.

I became present to my experience as it was, of being angry, frustrated, and impatient. I allowed these feelings fully.

I wrote:

> This is so frustrating. Doesn't she understand how important this is? I mean, how much more clearly can I communicate? I feel as if I've done my part of this 150%, and now I have

to do another 50% that I don't even have the information to complete? How is that okay? I just don't understand how she can't understand that this has to be of a certain quality, or it might as well not be done at all.

Then I asked myself if I was willing to see this from another perspective. The first few times my honest response was no, and so I wrote more, and in writing more I discovered how helpless and scared I was feeling (beyond being angry). I kept writing until I felt I had really mined what was true for me, and until I was interested in seeing if there was another way to view the situation. Then I moved on to exploring other possibilities.

I played around with looking at the situation in three different ways. Each generated different ideas and different possible actions. Here they are:

Qualities: Light, Open, Soft

> I know that it is hard to be patient, but you never know why something is delayed, why she is not getting back to you about this. I'm sure that something difficult is happening for her, because this is not like her. Send her care and compassion. Also, maybe this is being delayed for some larger reason. I bet that when it does happen, you'll see that the timing is perfect. We can only see the moment that we are in, so let's see how this plays out for the best. I'm sure that it will. Just be patient. She'll come through.

Qualities: Direct, Hard, Bright

> This is absolutely ridiculous. What kind of professionalism is this? I shouldn't have to work this hard to get her to do her job. I mean come on. I'm asking for one tiny action from her. It's not rocket science. I've even offered to do it myself. I should just lay down the law here. I mean really. She's obviously not responding to kindness.

Qualities: Wavy, Open, Shallow

> Um. This is hard. I don't know what to do. I think I'll take a nap.

So you can do this with any topic. Mine your own perspective, generate new ones, and then alchemize the wisdom of all of them.

You can alchemize in several different ways.

Key Points:

You can draw out the key points and possible actions.

For example, the key points from my initial perspective indicate that I need an action to be taken, and my upset feelings indicate that I care about it getting done quickly and well.

The first imaginative perspective is closest to my usual one: wait it out and look for the lesson.

You'll also notice that it is written in the third person. Sometimes that happens. Different perspectives speak differently, and in fact, neuroscientists have discovered that speaking in the third person helps calm brain activity and facilitates emotional regulation. ("You're okay, Eliza." Versus "I'm okay.")[123]

The second perspective's wisdom is to advocate and take action.

The third perspective is also wise in its way: Don't take an action when you feel under-resourced to take that action well.

So, in combining the wisdom from all of these, I can honor the fact that I need an action to be taken, but I can go about approaching it in a new way.

I can do something that helps me feel grounded and resourced (go for a run, take a walk, listen to some music, take a nap), so I am not lashing out from frustration or ruminating.

Then I can take a different communication action than I have taken so far. For example, I can call instead of emailing. And I don't have to lay down the law in that call. I can still extend curiosity and kindness even though I am more directly and boldly advocating for the task to be accomplished.

Together the three new perspectives give me more options to achieve my goal than I had with my default setting of sending emails while feeling frustrated and angry, and trying to be loving and patient.

Update:

I did take these actions in this way. I waited until I felt rested and then I called instead of emailing. In the phone call, I learned that my colleague was overwhelmed at work and had had a death in the family. She thanked me for calling and gave me the information I needed to finish the project.

Holding Space:

You can also read them back to yourself, holding all of the perspectives in your mind and self at once. You can set a timer for 5–10 minutes and sit with them. Or go for a walk with them in your awareness, and see what you notice.

Journaling:

You can read them back to yourself and then journal a stream of consciousness about what you read, and see what new insights occur to you. Three pages is the magic number.[124]

Shower Inspiration:

Don't give them another thought, and see what, if anything, comes to mind about the topic you are trying to solve at an unexpected moment.

Or you can do all of these.

Here is a template for you to use.

What is the issue? ....

What is my emotionally granular, honest response? What is really present for me?

Current perspective:...

Do I want to see this from another perspective? If yes then proceed. If no then stay with what is at hand:..

Choose a tool.

Generate three perspectives from that tool.

Perspective 1:...

Perspective 2:...

Perspective 3:...

Alchemize using key points, holding space, journaling, or shower inspiration.

New Insights:..

Enjoy!

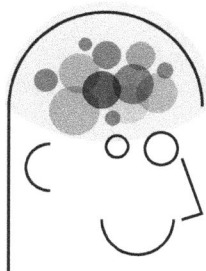

Glossary of Possibilities

Qualities

Light	Hard	Wavy	Wide
Heavy	Smooth	Still	Huge
Bright	Rough	Flat	Tiny
Dark	Clean	Round	Loud
Fast	Dusty	Direct	Quiet
Slow	Shallow	Indirect	Sparking
Soft	Deep	Narrow	Dull

Psychological Actions

Celebrate	Judge	Wonder	Flirt
Insult	Question	Ignore	Seduce
Welcome	Decide	Lambast	Whine
Reject	Ponder	Coddle	Complain
Bolster	Declare	Challenge	Suggest
Undermine	Avoid	Submit	
Accept	Face	Hide	

Internal Physical Actions[125]

Saunter	Gallop	Expand*	Flick**
Meander	Bulldoze	Push*	Dab**
Trudge	Sail	Pull*	Twirl
Sprint	Rush	Wring*	Glide
Tumble	Tip-toe	Smash*	Spear
Trip	Waddle	Toss	
Skip	Contract*	Heave	

Super-Objectives/Values

Power	Progress	Beauty	Truth
Money	Conservation	Fun	Adventure
Love	Justice	Pleasure	Efficiency
Friendship	Freedom	Legacy	Tradition
Service	Knowledge	Domination	Stability
Winning	Safety	Protection	
Peace	Transcendence	Loyalty	

Beliefs About the World

The world is safe	Things tend to work out
The world is unsafe	Things tend to not work out
The world is orderly	Resources are bounteous
The world is chaotic	Resources are scarce
The world is welcoming	Life is beautiful
The world is forbidding	Life is ugly
The world is a playground	Life is easy
The world is a prison	Life is hard

Beliefs About the Self

I am in control

I am powerless

I am very capable

I am not very capable

I am smart

I am stupid

I am attractive

I am ugly

I am better than other people

Other people are better than me

I am smarter than other people

Other people are smarter than me

I am a master

I am a servant

I am weak

I am strong

Beliefs About People in General

People are manipulative

People are honest

People are helpful

People are selfish

People are rational

People are irrational

People are capable

People are incapable

People are stewards

People are masters

People can change

People can't change

People are always responsible for their actions

People aren't always responsible for their actions

Some people are better than other people

No one is better than anyone else

Physicality

Eyes hardened

Eyes softened

Chin tucked in

Chin cocked

Shoulders forward

Shoulders back

Chest closed

Chest open

Arms crossed

Arms uncrossed

Elbows held close to the sides

Elbows relaxed away from the sides

Hands soft

Hand tensed

Active fingers

Still fingers

Stomach relaxed

Stomach held in

Pelvis tilted forward

Pelvis tucked back

Knees apart

Knees close together

Ankles angled

Ankles straight ahead

Weight toward balls of feet

Weight toward heels of feet

Inner Atmospheres

A sunny beach

A graveyard at night

A still lake

An amusement park

A mall

A dark wood-paneled office

A windowed, sleek, modern conference room

A used bookstore

A stormy night

A rap concert

A butterfly-filled meadow

A packed football stadium

A bombed-out building

A tornado

Early morning in summer

Late night at a club

A beige waiting room

A sterile laboratory

A cigarette-smoke-filled bar

A bed in a luxury hotel room

An old farmhouse porch in spring

A trashcan filled back-alley at night

An empty green tiled bathtub

Crisp autumn leaves falling

Bubble gum pink roller skating rink

A bright, joyful preschool classroom

Endnotes

1   Herbert Barber, "Developing Strategic Leadership: The U.S. Army War College Experience", *Journal of Management Development*, Vol. 11 No. 6. (1992): pp. 4-12

2   "Who first originated the term VUCA (Volatility, Uncertainty, Complexity and Ambiguity)?" U.S. Army Heritage and Information Center, at Carlisle Barracks. (May 7, 2019). Last retrieved 7/24/2019 http://www.usawc.libanswers.com/faq/84869

3   Albert Einstein, *On Cosmic Religion and Other Opinions & Aphorisms* (Dover Publications; Dover edition, 2009) p. 104

4   "Interview with Sally Field: Promoting Healthy Habits." *Ability Magazine.* (2009) Last retrieved 7/24/2019 https://abilitymagazine.com/past/sallyF/sallyF.html

5   Alan Turing, *Systems of Logic Based on Ordinals*. [PhD Dissertation, Princeton University] (1938) p. 106

6   Lincoln Kinnear Barnett, "The Universe and Dr. Einstein." *Harper's Magazine.* (April, 1948)

7   M. Rangel-Gomez, C. Hickey, T. van Amelsvoort, P. Bet, and M. Meeter, "The detection of novelty relies on dopaminergic signaling: evidence from apomorphine's impact on the novelty N2." *PLoS One.* (2013) 2013;8(6):e66469

8   Jacqueline Whitt [Host], "Is "VUCA" a useful term or is it all "vuca'ed up?" *The War Room.* (2018, July 13) [Audio podcast] Last retrieved 7/24/2019 https://warroom.armywarcollege.edu/podcasts/is-vuca-useful/

9   Sherry Kramer, *David's RedHaired Death.* (New York: Broadway Play Company, 2012) First produced by Wooly Mammoth Theater Company 1990–1991 season. Excerpt used with generous permission of the playwright.

10   David Rock, "Hunger for Certainty: Your brain craves certainty and avoids uncertainty like it's pain." *Psychology Today.* (2009, October 25). Last retrieved 7/24/2019 https://www.psychologytoday.com/us/blog/your-brain-work/200910/hunger-certainty

11   John Tierney, "What's New? Exuberance for Novelty Has Benefits." *New York Times.* (February 13, 2012)

12   You can learn more about Dr. C Robert Cloninger's work at the Center for Well-Being, the home of the Temperament and Character Inventory. Last retrieved 7/24/2019 https://tcipersonality.com/

13   Terry Gross [Host], "Interview with Annette Benning: Acting is 'A fabulous way to expand your own heart.'" *Fresh Air* [Radio program] (May 10, 2018) Last retrieved 7/24/2019 https://www.npr.org/2018/05/10/610014961/annette-bening-acting-is-a-fabulous-way-to-expand-your-own-heart

14   *"Crazy," Lexico,* [Oxford Dictionary.] Last retrieved 8/28/2019 www.lexico.com/en/definition/crazy

15   Plato, *Theaetetus.* [155d.] The original quote is "wonder is the only beginning of philosophy," but the meaning is more toward "wonder is the beginning of wisdom" because the word "philosophy" has its etymology in philo- "love" and sophy- "wisdom." So, Plato would have meant it more thusly.

16   Alice Walker, *The Color Purple.* (Harcourt Brace Jovanovich, 1982) Part 5, p. 247

17   Constantine Stanislavski, *Creating a Role.* (New York: Routledge, 1989) p. 5

18   Bill Davidow, "Exploiting the Neuroscience of Internet Addiction." *The Atlantic* (July 18, 2012) Last retrieved 7/25/2019 https://www.theatlantic.com/health/archive/2012/07/exploiting-the-neuroscience-of-internet-addiction/259820/

19   Daniel Nettle, *Personality: What Makes You the Way You Are* (New York: Oxford University Press, 2007)

20   Emrah Düzel, Nico Bunzek, "Absolute Coding of Stimulus Novelty in the Human Substantia Nigra/VTA'" *Neuron* (August 3, 2006.) doi.org/10.1016/j.neuron.2006.06.021

Tianna Hicklin, "How novelty boosts memory retention." *National Institutes of Health.* (September 20, 2016) Last retrieved 7/25/2019 https://www.nih.gov/news-events/nih-research-matters/how-novelty-boosts-memory-retention

21   Stephen Fortune, "Why psychological safety is the key to creativity and innovation in the workplace." *The Oxford Group.* (April 30, 2018) Last retrieved 7/25/2019 https://www.oxford-group.com/insights/why-psychological-safety-key-creativity-and-innovation-workplace

Laura Delizonna, "High-Performing Teams Need Psychological Safety. Here's How to Create It." *Harvard Business Review.* (August 24, 2017) Last retrieved 7/25/2019 https://hbr.org/2017/08/high-performing-teams-need-psychological-safety-heres-how-to-create-it

22   If this is interesting to you, you can explore further through Barbara Fredrickson's work at Pep Lab at UNC Chapel Hill. Last retrieved 7/25/2019 http://peplab.web.unc.edu/research/#broadenandbuild

23   L. J. Levine and R. S. Edelstein, "Emotion and memory narrowing: A review and goal-relevance approach." Cognition and Emotion. (2009). 23, 833–875. DOI: 10.1080/02699930902738863

24   E. A. Kensinger and S. Corkin, "Memory enhancement for emotional words: Are emotional words more vividly remembered than neutral words?" Memory & Cognition. (December, 2003) 31,1169–1180. DOI: 10.3758/BF03195800

25   Kurt Matzler, Franz Bailom, and Todd Mooradian, "Intuitive Decision Making." MIT Sloan Management Review 49.1 (Fall, 2007): 13–15 Last retrieved 7/25/2019 https://sloanreview.mit.edu/article/intuitive-decision-making/

26   IMDB James Dean, Quotes Last retrieved 7/25/2019 https://m.imdb.com/name/nm0000015/quotes

27   Carol Kinsey Goman, "Seven Seconds to Make a First Impression." *Forbes.* (2011) last retrieved 8/26/2019 https://www.forbes.com/sites/carolkinseygoman/2011/02/13/seven-seconds-to-make-a-first-impression/#230682b82722

Shannon Polly, "First Impressions – the 7/11 Rule." *Positive Business DC.*(2015) retrieved 8/26/2019 http://positivebusinessdc.com/711-rule/

Rik, "The Relationship Edge: Your first 7 seconds are critical." *Life Beyond Limits* (2017). https://lifebeyondlimits.com.au/relationships-edge/

28   For a good, easy description of Confirmation Bias see "Confirmation Bias." *Encyclopedia Britannica Online.* Last retrieved 7/25/2019. https://www.britannica.com/science/confirmation-bias

29   Robert Kriegel and David Brandt, Sacred Cows Make The Best Burgers, *Sacred Cows Make the Best Burgers: Developing Change-Driving People and Organizations.* (New York: Warner, 1997) p. 42

30   Donald K. Freedheim (editor), *Handbook of Psychology, History of Psychology* (New Jersey: John Wiley & Sons, Inc, 2003) p. 57

31   C. Anderson, D. Keltner, and O. P. John, "Emotional convergence between people over time." *Journal of Personality and Social Psychology.* (2003) Vol. 84, No. 5, pp. 1054–1068

S. Barsade, "The Ripple Effect: Emotional Contagion and Its Influence on Group Behavior." *Administrative Science Quarterly.* (2002) Vol. 47, pp. 644–675

A. Hatfield, J. Cacioppo, and R. L. Rapson *Emotional contagion.* (Cambridge, UK: Cambridge University Press, 1994)

L. Lundqvist and U. Dimberg, "Facial expressions are contagious." *Journal of Psychophysiology.* (1990) Vol. 9, pp. 203–211

32   If this is interesting to you, please look at Sigal Barsade's work out of the Wharton School of Management. Last retrieved 7/25/2019 https://mgmt.wharton.upenn.edu/profile/barsade/#research

33   For a clear, easy description of emotional contagion please visit "Emotional Contagion" at iresearchnet. Last retrieved 7/25/2019 https://psychology.iresearchnet.com/social-psychology/emotions/emotional-contagion/

34   Tjerk Mollac, Geir Jordet B & Gert-Jan Peppinga, "Emotional contagion in soccer penalty shootouts: Celebration of individual success is associated with ultimate team success." *Journal of Sports Sciences.* (2010) 28:9, pp. 983–992, DOI: 10.1080/02640414.2010.484068

35   Joel S. Milner, Lea B. Halsey, and Jim Fultz, "Empathic responsiveness and affective reactivity to infant stimuli in high- and low-risk for physical child abuse mothers." *Child Abuse and Neglect: The International Journal.* (June, 1995) Vol. 19, Issue: 6; pp. 659–784 doi.org/10.1016/0145-2134(95)00035-7

36   Chen-Bo Zhong, "Cold and Lonely: Does Social Exclusion Literally Feel Cold?" *Association for Psychological Science* (2008) 19:9 Last retrieved 7/25/2019 https://www.psychologicalscience.org/news/releases/cold-and-lonely-does-social-exclusion-literally-feel-cold.html

37   Joshua Aronson, Michael J. Lustina, Catherine Good, Kelli Keough, Claude M. Steele, and Joseph Brown, "When White Men Can't Do Math: Necessary and Sufficient Factors in Stereotype Threat." Journal of Experimental Social Psychology. (1999) 35:1; 29-46 doi.org/10.1006/jesp.1998.1371

38   Brett W. Pelham, Matthew C. Mirenberg, and John T. Jones, "Why Susie Sells Seashells by the Seashore: Implicit Egotism and Major Life Decisions." *The Journal of Attitudes and Cognition.* (2002) 82(4), pp. 469–487. doi.org/10.1037/0022-3514.82.4.469

39   Michael Billig and Henri Tajfel, "Social categorization and similarity in intergroup behavior." *European Journal of Social Psychology.* (1973) 3:1; pp. 27–52 https://doi.org/10.1002/ejsp.2420030103

If this is interesting to you, the citations in the following article are especially interesting: Anne Locksley, Christine Hepburn and Vilma Ortiz, "Social stereotypes and judgments of individuals: An instance of the base-rate fallacy." *Journal of Experimental Social Psychology* (1982) 18:1

40   Marco Iacoboni, *Mirroring People: The Science of Empathy and How We Connect with Others.* (New York: Picador, 2009)

41   David Eagleman, *Incognito: The Secret Lives of The Brain.* (New York: Random House, 2011) p. 48

42   Omniglot: The Online Dictionary of Writing Systems and Languages, "Pali" entry. Last retrieved 7/25/2019 https://www.omniglot.com/writing/pali.htm

43   David Eagleman, *Incognito: The Secret Lives of The Brain.* (New York: Random House, 2011) p. 42

44   Robert Sapolsky, *Behave: The Biology of Humans at Our Best and Worst.* (New York: Penguin Books, 2017) p. 78

45   Simone G. Shamay-Tsoory, Dorin Ahronberg-Kirschenbaum, and Nirit Bauminger-Zviely, "There Is No Joy Like Malicious Joy: Schadenfreude in Young Children." *PLoS ONE.* (July 2, 2014) doi.org/10.1371/journal.pone.0100233

46   Alexander Strobel et al, "Beyond Revenge: Neural and Genetic Bases of Altruistic Punishment." *NeuroImage.* (2011) 54(1), pp. 671–680 doi.org/10.1016/j.neuroimage.2010.07.051

47   Marco Brambilla and Paolo Riva, "Selfimage and Schadenfreude: Pleasure at Others' Misfortune Enhances Satisfaction of Basic Human Needs." *European Journal of Social Psychology.* (2017) 47, pp. 399–411. DOI: 10.1002/ejsp.2229

48   Daniel Goleman, *Destructive Emotions: A Scientific Dialogue with the Dalai Lama.* (New York: Bantam, 2004) p. 148

49   Jill Bolte Taylor, *My Stroke of Insight.* (New York: Viking Penguin, 2008) p. 146

50   "Billionaire Ray Dalio credits meditation for success." *TM Home: Transcendental Meditation, News and More.* (November 28, 2014). Last retrieved 7/24/2019 https://tmhome.com/experiences/billionaire-ray-dalio-on-benefits-of-meditation/

51   Course: *u.lab: Leading From the Emerging Future, MIT* Last retrieved 7/26/2019 https://www.edx.org/course/ulab-leading-from-the-emerging-future

52   Anne Murphy Paul, "It's Not Me, It's You," *New York Times: Sunday Review.* (October 6, 2012) Last retrieved 8/1/2019 https://www.nytimes.com/2012/10/07/opinion/sunday/intelligence-and-the-stereotype-threat.html

53   Written by Kimberly Holland [written by] with Timothy J. Legg [medically reviewed by], "Intrusive Thoughts: Why We Have Them and How to Stop Them." *Healthline.* Last retrieved 7/26/2019 https://www.healthline.com/health/mental-health/intrusive-thoughts

54   Joshua Freedman, "Before Your Meeting: A Profoundly Simple Question." *Six Seconds EQ Business* (September 5, 2012) Last retrieved 7/26/2019 https://www.6seconds.org/2012/09/05/before-your-meeting-a-profoundly-simple-question/

55   See Barbara Fredrickson's work Pep Lab at UNC Chapel Hill. Last retrieved 7/25/2019 http://peplab.web.unc.edu/research/#broadenandbuild

56   Daniel Nettle, *Personality: What Makes You the Way You Are.* p. 122

57   Jordi Quoidbach, June Gruber, Moïra Mikolajczak, et al., "Emodiversity and the Emotional Ecosystem." *Journal of Experimental Psychology. General.* (2014). 143(6):2066. DOI: 10.1037/a0038025

58   Katharine E. Smidt, and Michael K. Suvak, "A Brief, But Nuanced, Review of Emotional Granularity and Emotion Differentiation Research." *Current Opinion in Psychology.* (2015) V. 3 pp. 48–51 doi.org/10.1016/j. copsyc.2015.02.007

59   Lisa Feldman Barrett, *How Emotions Are Made: The Secret Life of the Brain.* (New York: Houghton Mifflin Harcourt, 2017) p. 180

60   Krista Tippett [host], "Interview with Mahzarin Banaji The Mind is a Difference Seeking Machine," *On Being.* (2018). Last retrieved on 7/26/2018 https://onbeing.org/programs/mahzarin-banaji-the-mind-is-a-difference-seeking-machine-aug2018/#transcript

61   https://www.goodreads.com/author/quotes/5943.Desmond_Tutu

62   Theo E.J. Wilson, *A black man goes undercover with the alt-right.* TEDxMileHigh (2017) Last retrieved 8/22/2019 https://www.ted.com/talks/theo_e_j_wilson_a_black_man_goes_undercover_in_the_alt_right

Scott Taylor, "Rethinking What We Think About How to Change." *TEDx Babson College* (2019). Last retrieved 7/25/2019 https://www.youtube.com/watch?v=FClv1h4L1H8

63   Viktor Frankl, "Youth in Search of Meaning." *Toronto Youth Corps.* (1972) Last retrieved 7/26/2019 https://logotherapy.univie.ac.at/clipgallery.html

64   Albert, Einstein. (1931) *On Cosmic Religion and Other Opinions and Aphorisms.* (Dover Publications; Dover edition, 2009) p. 5

65   Yuval Noah Harari, "What Explains the Rise of Humans," *TEDGlobalLondon* (2015) Last retrieved 7/26/2019 https://www.ted.com/talks/yuval_noah_harari_what_explains_the_rise_of_humans/transcript?language=en

66   J. K. Norem and N. Cantor, "Defensive pessimism: harnessing anxiety as motivation." *Journal of Personality and Social Psychology.* (1986) 51(6): pp. 1208–17. PMID: 3806357

67   Marco Iacoboni, *Mirroring People: The Science of Empathy and How We Connect with Others.* (New York: Picador, 2009)

68   Meryl Streep, "Quotes", *IMDB* Last retrieved 7/26/2019 https://www.imdb.com/name/nm0000658/bio?ref_=nm_dyk_qt_sm#quotes

69   Will Gompertz [host], "Dame Judi Dench on Queen Victoria, love and her favourite roles." [Audio] *BBC.* (2017) Last retrieved 7/26/2019 https://www.bbc.com/news/av/entertainment-arts-41089305/dame-judi-dench-on-queen-victoria-love-and-her-favourite-roles

70   J.K. Rowling, "'The Fringe Benefits of Failure, and the Importance of Imagination." *Harvard Commencement Address* (2008) Last retrieved 7/26/2019 https://news.harvard.edu/gazette/story/2008/06/text-of-j-k-rowling-speech/

71   Gabriele Oettingen, Hyeon-ju Pak and Karoline Schnetter, "Self-Regulation of Goal Setting: Turning Free Fantasies About the Future Into Binding Goals." *Journal of Personality and Social Psychology* (2001) 80:5; pp. 736–753 DOI: 1O.1037//O022-3514.80.5.736

72   Heidi Grant Halvorson, *Suceed: How We Can Reach Our Goals: 9 Things Successful People Do Differently*. (New York: Penguin, 2010)

73   Robert Dielenberg and Iain Mcgregor, "Defensive behavior in rats towards predatory odors: A review." *Neuroscience and Biobehavioral Reviews*. (2001). 25. pp. 597–609. 10.1016/S0149-7634(01)00044-6

74   Meeri Kim, "Study finds that fear can travel quickly through generations of mice DNA." *Washington Post*. (December 7, 2013) Last retrieved 7/27/19 https://www.washingtonpost.com/national/health-science/study-finds-that-fear-can-travel-quickly-through-generations-of-mice-dna/2013/12/07/94dc97f2-5e8e-11e3-bc56-c6ca94801fac_story.html

Brian G. Dias & Kerry J. Ressler, "Parental olfactory experience influences behavior and neural structure in subsequent generations." *Nature Neuroscience*. (2014) volume 17, pp. 89–96 Last retrieved 8/26/2019 DOI: 10.1038/nn.3594

75   Signe Dean, "Scientists Have Observed Epigenetic Memories Being Passed Down For 14 Generations." *Science Alert*. (April 27, 2018) Last retrieved 7/27/19 https://www.sciencealert.com/scientists-observe-epigenetic-memories-passed-down-for-14-generations-most-animal

Center for Genomic Regulation, "Environmental 'memories' passed on for 14 generations." *Science Daily*. (20 April 2017). Last retrieved 8/26//2019 www.sciencedaily.com/releases/2017/04/170420141753.htm

76   Sonja Lyubomirsky, *The How of Happiness: A New Approach to Getting the Life You Want*. (New York: Penguin, 2007) p. 92

77   Daniel Nettle, *Personality: What Makes You the Way You Are* (New York: Oxford University Press, 2007) p. 239

78   John J. Ratey, *A User's Guide to the Brain: Perception, Attention, and the Four Theaters of the Brain*. (New York: Random House, 2002) p. 36

79   Gore Vidal, *Julian, a novel*. (New York: Random House, 1962) p. 56

80   Jeremy Dean, *Making Habits, Breaking Habits: How to Make Changes that Stick*. (Boston: Da Capo Press, 2013) p. 158

81   William Shakespeare, *Hamlet*. Act II, Sc ii

82   Daniel Goleman, *Emotional Intelligence: Why It Can Matter More Than IQ.* (New York: Bantam, 1995) p. 22

Also, if this is interesting to you please see Joseph LeDoux's work.

83   John H. Riskind, "They Stoop to Conquer: Guiding and self-regulatory functions of physical posture after success and failure." *Journal of Personality and Social Psychology.* (1984) Vol 47:3; pp. 479–493. DOI: 10.1037/0022-3514.47.3.479

84   J. P. Forgas, L. Goldenberg, and C. Unkelbach, "Can bad weather improve your memory? An unobtrusive field study of natural mood effects on real-life memory." *Journal of Experimental Social Psychology.* (2009) 54, pp. 254–257. DOI:10.1016/j.jesp.2008.08.014

85   "Thinking negatively can boost your memory, study finds." *Reuters.* (November 2, 2009) https://www.reuters.com/article/idUSSP488505

86   Chandrika Tandon [host], "Ancient Wisdom in Modern Times – Deepak Chopra and Sadhguru, moderated by Ms. Chandrika Tandon." *Conference of Bharath Vidhya Bhavan, Pierre Hotel, New York Published by Inner Engineering. (2015)* Last retrieved 7/30/2019 https://www.youtube.com/watch?time_continue=2647&v=WMhJgdpj1d0

87   "William James," *University of Kentucky.* Last retrieved 7/30/2019 https://www.uky.edu/~eushe2/quotations/james.html

88   "Jon Kabat-Zinn: Defining Mindfulness. What is mindfulness? The founder of Mindfulness-Based Stress Reduction Explains." *Mindful Magazine.* (January 11, 2017) Last retrieved 7/28/2019 https://www.mindful.org/jon-kabat-zinn-defining-mindfulness

89   Ellen J. Langer, "Mindful Learning." *Current directions in psychological science.* (2000) 9:6; pp. 220–223. doi.org/10.1111/1467-8721.00099

90   Ellen J. Langer, *Mindfulness.* (Boston: Da Capo, 1989) p. 150

91   Alia J. Crum, and Ellen J. Langer, "Mind-set matters: Exercise and the Placebo Effect." *Psychological Science.* (2007) 18:2; 165–171. DOI:10.1111/j.1467-9280.2007.01867.x

92   Scott R. Bishop, et al., "Mindfulness: A Proposed Operational Definition." Clinical Psychology: Science and Practice. (2004). 11:3; 230–241. DOI:10.1093/clipsy/bph077

93   Wendy Wood, "Habit in Personality and Social Psychology." *Personality and Social Psychology Review.* (November, 2017). 21:4; 389–403. DOI:10.1177/1088868317720362

94   "Capitalizing on Complexity: Insights from the Global Chief Executive Officer Study." *IBM.* Last retrieved 7/28/2019 https://www.ibm.com/downloads/cas/1VZV5X8J

95   Albert Rothenberg, "The Process of Janusian Thinking in Creativity." *Archives of General Psychology*. (1971) 24:3; 195 DOI:10.1001/archpsyc.1971.01750090001001

96   Valerie Strauss, "The surprising thing Google learned about its employees — and what it means for today's students." *The Washington Post*. (December 20, 2017) Last retrieved 7/28/2019 https://www.washingtonpost.com/news/answer-sheet/wp/2017/12/20/the-surprising-thing-google-learned-about-its-employees-and-what-it-means-for-todays-students/

97   David Comer Kidd and Emanuele Castano, "Reading Fiction Improves Theory of Mind." *Science*. (2013). 342:6156; pp. 377–380 DOI: 10.1126/science.1239918

98   Annie Leonard, *The Story of Stuff* [Short film] The Story of Stuff Project (2007)

99   Liz Mineo, "Good genes are nice but joy is better." *The Harvard Gazette*. (2017) Last retrieved 7/29/2019 https://news.harvard.edu/gazette/story/2017/04/over-nearly-80-years-harvard-study-has-been-showing-how-to-live-a-healthy-and-happy-life/

100   Rachel Rettner, "Want to Live Longer? Get Some Friends." *LiveScience*. (July 27, 2010) Last retrieved 7/28/2019 https://www.livescience.com/6769-live-longer-friends.html

101   Sachin Jain, "A Treatment for Loneliness: Can a physician write a prescription for friendship?" *Harvard Medicine*. Last retrieved 7/26/2019 https://hms.harvard.edu/magazine/imaging/treatment-loneliness

102   Katharine Gammon, "Why Loneliness Can Be Deadly." *LiveScience*. (March, 2012). Last retrieved 7/26/2019 https://www.livescience.com/18800-loneliness-health-problems.html

Jessica Lahey and Tim Lahey, "How Loneliness Wears on the Body: New research supports the idea that social isolation is detrimental to physical health— and that companionship may improve it." *The Atlantic*. (December, 2015) Last retrieved 8/26/2019 https://www.theatlantic.com/health/archive/2015/12/loneliness-social-isolation-and-health/418395/

103   Kirsten Weir, "The pain of social rejection: As far as the brain is concerned, a broken heart may not be so different from a broken arm." *American Psychological Association*. (April, 2012) 43:4; p. 50.

Naomi I. Eisenberger, Matthew D. Lieberman, and Kipling D. Williams, "Does Rejection Hurt? An fMRI Study of Social Exclusion." *Science* (2003) 302:5643; pp. 290–292 DOI: 10.1126/science.10891.

Last retrieved 8/26/2019 https://www.researchgate.net/publication/9056800_Does_Rejection_Hurt_An_fMRI_Study_of_Social_Exclusion

104   Sam Harris, "Drugs and the Meaning of Life." *Making Sense with Sam Harris*. [Podcast] Last retrieved https://www.youtube.com/watch?v=SQO2552UJko

105   Viola Spolin, *Improvisation for the Theater: A Handbook of Teaching and Directing Techniques*. (Illinois: Northwestern University Press, 1963) p. 3

106   Daniel Goleman, "The Sweet Spot for Achievement: What's the relationship between stress and performance?" *Psychology Today.* (March, 2012) Last retrieved 7/26/2019 https://www.psychologytoday.com/au/blog/the-brain-and-emotional-intelligence/201203/the-sweet-spot-achievement

107   J. Kiverstein, and M. Miller, "The embodied brain: towards a radical embodied cognitive neuroscience." *Frontiers in Human Neuroscience.* (May, 2015) doi.org/10.3389/fnhum.2015.00237

R. Levenson, P. Ekman, and W. Friesen, W, "Voluntary Facial Action Generates Emotion-Specific Autonomic Nervous System Activity." *Psychophysiology* (1990) 27:4; pp. 363–384 doi.org/10.1111/j.1469-8986.1990.tb02330.x

George Wigmore, "Research shows that smiling affects the way our brains process other people's emotions." *MedicalXpress.* (2015) Last retrieved 8/26/201 https://medicalxpress.com/news/2015-06-affects-brains-people-emotions.html

108   N. H. Frijda, *The Emotions*. (Cambridge: Cambridge University Press, 1986)

109   Shlomo Hareli, Konstantinos Kafetsios, and Ursula Hess, "A cross-cultural study on emotion expression and the learning of social norms." *Frontiers in Psychology*, (October, 2015) https://doi.org/10.3389/fpsyg.2015.01501

110   If this is interesting to you please see Paul Ekman's work https://www.paulekman.com/paul-ekman/

111   Edgar Allan Poe, *The Purloined Letter.* (CreateSpace Independent Publishing Platform, 2015). p. 30

112   If this is interesting to you, please look at Sigal Barsade's work out of the Wharton School of Management. Last retrieved 7/25/2019 https://mgmt.wharton.upenn.edu/profile/barsade/#research

113   Frank Pierce Jones, *Freedom to Change: the development and science of the Alexander Technique.* (London: Mouritz, 1997) p. 3

114   Walt Whitman, *Song of Myself.* (1892)

115   Kurt Fischer and Thomas Bidell, "Dynamic Development of Action and Thought." In W. Damon and R. M. Lerner (Eds.) *Theoretical Models of Human Development. Handbook of Child Psychology.* (New York, Wiley, 2006) p. 318

116   "Are You Facing a Problem? Or a Polarity?" *Center for Creative Leadership.* Last retrieved 7/26/2019 https://www.ccl.org/articles/leading-effectively-articles/are-you-facing-a-problem-or-a-polarity/

117   Howard, Thurman, *The Search For Common Ground: An Inquiry Into The Basis Of Man's Experience Of Community.* (Harper Row Publishers, 1971) p. 104

118   Max Ernst [site] Last retrieved 8/26/2019 http://www.max-ernst.com/quotes.jsp

119   Chimamanda Ngozi Adichie, "The Danger of a Single Story." *TEDGlobal 2009* Last retrieved 7/28/2019 https://www.ted.com/talks/chimamanda_adichie_the_danger_of_a_single_story

120   And, as an aside, this is the full passage, which you might enjoy, in a translation by Kwame Anthony Appiah (*Cosmopolitanism: Ethics in a World of Strangers [Issues of Our Time]*), (New York: Norton, 2006) pp. 111–113:

"I am human: nothing human is alien to me. Either I want to find out for myself or I want to advise you: think what you like. If you're right, I'll do what you do. If you're wrong, I'll set you straight." – Terence, *Heauton Timorumenos (translation The Self-Tormenter)*.

121   Henri Tajfel, M. G. Billig. R. P. Bundy, and Claude Flament, "Social categorization and intergroup behavior." *European Journal of Social Psychology.* (1971) 1:2; 149–178 https://doi.org/10.1002/ejsp.2420010202

122   David J. Hargreaves, Andrew M. Colman, and Wladyslaw Sluckin, "The Attractiveness of Names." *Human Relations.* (1983) 36:4; 393–402

Anushka Asthana, "Names really do make a difference: Research shows that girls with 'feminine' names steer clear of 'masculine' maths and science." *The Guardian.* (2007) Last retrieved 7/28/2019 www.guardian.co.uk/science/2007/apr/29/theobserversuknewspages.uknews

Joe Brownstein, "Does Your Name Determine Your Destiny?" *LiveScience.* (2011) Last retrieved 8/26/2019 https://www.livescience.com/13477-names-life-decisions-career-choices.html

123   Christopher Bergland, "Silent Third Person Self-Talk Facilitates Emotion Regulation: Try using your own name during inner dialogues." *Psychology Today.* (July 28, 2017) Last retrieved 7/28/2019 https://www.psychologytoday.com/gb/blog/the-athletes-way/201707/silent-third-person-self-talk-facilitates-emotion-regulation

Michigan State University, "Talking to yourself in the third person can help you control emotions." *Science Daily.* (July 26, 2017) Last retrieved 7/28/2019 https://www.sciencedaily.com/releases/2017/07/170726102906.htm

Fritz Strack, Leonard Martin, Sabine Stepper, "Inhibiting and Facilitating Conditions of the Human Smile: A Nonobtrusive Test of the Facial Feedback Hypothesis." *Journal of Personality and Social Psychology.* (1988) 54: 5; pp. 768–777 DOI: 10.1037//0022-3514.54.5.768

124   Julia Cameron, *The Artist's Way: A Spiritual Path to Higher Creativity.* (New York: Penguin, 1992)

125   Some of these words come from the work of Rudolph Laban** and Michael Chekhov*

126   William James, "Confidences of a 'Psychical Researcher'." *The American Magazine.* (1909). Vol. 68 p. 589 Last retrieved 7/27/2019 https://library.harvard.edu/onlineexhibits/james/psychical/7_8.html

Acknowledgments

I would like to deeply thank all of my students, and all of my explicit and implicit teachers. Also, each of you early-adopter supporters who preordered the book. Thank you! And to all of the thinkers and researchers whose work I have learned from, deepest gratitude and humblest thanks.

Also, I extend endless gratitude to Kirk Daffner, Marianne Dolan, Mindy Gibbins-Klein, Brit Lay, Michael Levine, Mary McLaughlin, Ray Munro, Wendolín Perla, Patrick Ryan (especially Patrick Ryan), Ann Seelye, Jack McCarthy, and Sally Taylor. Also, I have so much gratitude for the teams at Panoma and Publishizer. Thank you.

> Out of my experience, such as it is (and it is limited enough) one fixed conclusion dogmatically emerges, and that is this, that we with our lives are like islands in the sea, or like trees in the forest. The maple and the pine may whisper to each other with their leaves... But the trees also commingle their roots in the darkness underground, and the islands also hang together through the ocean's bottom. Just so there is a continuum of cosmic consciousness, against which our individuality builds but accidental fences.
>
> — William James[126]

About The Author

A speaker, teacher, and performing artist, Eliza Lay Ryan (MFA and CYT) has led acting programs and taught supermindfulness practices to people from all over the world. She collaborates in teaching and researching with leaders in neuroscience, business, wellness, and education.

She has been teaching, collaborating, and creating for the past 15 years, earning her Masters in Fine Arts in Theater and a 250-hour Yoga Teacher Certification. She acts, directs, choreographs, and combines her backgrounds in the arts, science, education, and wellness to offer practical, fun, intuitive practices and frameworks that allow people to access greater empathy, creativity, and wholeness in the flow of their daily lives.

She currently lives in the U.S. with her two largest fonts of inspiration, her husband and daughter.

www.ingramcontent.com/pod-product-compliance
Lightning Source LLC
Chambersburg PA
CBHW021400090426
42742CB00009B/933